HEALTH CARE IN TRANSITION

KEY ISSUES FACING MEDICAID

HEALTH CARE IN TRANSITION

Additional books in this series can be found on Nova's website under the Series tab.

Additional e-books in this series can be found on Nova's website under the e-book tab.

HEALTH CARE IN TRANSITION

KEY ISSUES FACING MEDICAID

JIMMY PHILLIPS
EDITOR

New York

Copyright © 2016 by Nova Science Publishers, Inc.

All rights reserved. No part of this book may be reproduced, stored in a retrieval system or transmitted in any form or by any means: electronic, electrostatic, magnetic, tape, mechanical photocopying, recording or otherwise without the written permission of the Publisher.

We have partnered with Copyright Clearance Center to make it easy for you to obtain permissions to reuse content from this publication. Simply navigate to this publication's page on Nova's website and locate the "Get Permission" button below the title description. This button is linked directly to the title's permission page on copyright.com. Alternatively, you can visit copyright.com and search by title, ISBN, or ISSN.

For further questions about using the service on copyright.com, please contact:
Copyright Clearance Center
Phone: +1-(978) 750-8400   Fax: +1-(978) 750-4470   E-mail: info@copyright.com.

NOTICE TO THE READER

The Publisher has taken reasonable care in the preparation of this book, but makes no expressed or implied warranty of any kind and assumes no responsibility for any errors or omissions. No liability is assumed for incidental or consequential damages in connection with or arising out of information contained in this book. The Publisher shall not be liable for any special, consequential, or exemplary damages resulting, in whole or in part, from the readers' use of, or reliance upon, this material. Any parts of this book based on government reports are so indicated and copyright is claimed for those parts to the extent applicable to compilations of such works.

Independent verification should be sought for any data, advice or recommendations contained in this book. In addition, no responsibility is assumed by the publisher for any injury and/or damage to persons or property arising from any methods, products, instructions, ideas or otherwise contained in this publication.

This publication is designed to provide accurate and authoritative information with regard to the subject matter covered herein. It is sold with the clear understanding that the Publisher is not engaged in rendering legal or any other professional services. If legal or any other expert assistance is required, the services of a competent person should be sought. FROM A DECLARATION OF PARTICIPANTS JOINTLY ADOPTED BY A COMMITTEE OF THE AMERICAN BAR ASSOCIATION AND A COMMITTEE OF PUBLISHERS.

Additional color graphics may be available in the e-book version of this book.

Library of Congress Cataloging-in-Publication Data

ISBN: 978-1-63484-647-9

Published by Nova Science Publishers, Inc. † New York

CONTENTS

Preface		**vii**
Chapter 1	Medicaid: Key Issues Facing the Program *United States Government Accountability Office*	**1**
Chapter 2	Background Memo for the Hearing on "Medicaid at 50: Strengthening and Sustaining the Program" *Staff of the House Committee on* *Energy and Commerce*	**87**
Chapter 3	Statement of Vikki Wachino, Deputy Administrator and Director, Center for Medicaid and CHIP Services, Centers for Medicare and Medicaid Services. Hearing on "Medicaid at 50: Strengthening and Sustaining the Program"	**97**
Chapter 4	Statement of Anne Schwartz, Executive Director, Medicaid and CHIP Payment and Access Commission (MACPAC). Hearing on "Medicaid at 50: Strengthening and Sustaining the Program"	**115**
Index		**121**

PREFACE

The Medicaid program marked its 50th anniversary on July 30, 2015. The joint federal-state program has grown to be one of the largest sources of health care coverage and financing for a diverse low-income and medically needy population. Medicaid is undergoing transformative changes, in part due to PPACA, which expanded the program by allowing states to opt to cover low-income adults in addition to individuals in historic categories, such as children, pregnant women, older adults, and individuals with disabilities. This book describes key issues that face the Medicaid program based on this work, and program and other changes with implications for federal oversight.

In: Key Issues Facing Medicaid
Editor: Jimmy Phillips

ISBN: 978-1-63484-647-9
© 2016 Nova Science Publishers, Inc.

Chapter 1

MEDICAID: KEY ISSUES FACING THE PROGRAM[*]

United States Government Accountability Office

WHY GAO DID THIS STUDY

The Medicaid program marks its 50th anniversary on July 30, 2015. The joint federal-state program has grown to be one of the largest sources of health care coverage and financing for a diverse low-income and medically needy population. Medicaid is undergoing transformative changes, in part due to PPACA, which expanded the program by allowing states to opt to cover low-income adults in addition to individuals in historic categories, such as children, pregnant women, older adults, and individuals with disabilities.

GAO has a large body of work on challenges facing Medicaid and gaps in federal oversight. This report describes (1) key issues that face the Medicaid program based on this work, and (2) program and other changes with implications for federal oversight. GAO reviewed its reports on Medicaid issued from January 2005 through July 2015; reviewed documentation from the Centers for Medicare & Medicaid Services (CMS), the HHS agency that oversees Medicaid; and interviewed CMS officials.

---

[*] This is an edited, reformatted and augmented version of the United States Government Accountability Office publication, GAO-15-677, dated July 2015.

WHAT GAO RECOMMENDS

GAO has made over 80 recommendations regarding Medicaid, some of which HHS has implemented. GAO has highlighted 24 key recommendations that have not been implemented. HHS agreed with and is acting on some and did not agree with others. GAO continues to believe that all of its recommendations have merit and should be implemented. HHS provided technical comments on a draft of this report, which GAO incorporated as appropriate.

WHAT GAO FOUND

GAO identified four key issues facing the Medicaid program, based on prior work.

- **Access to care**: Medicaid enrollees report access to care that is generally comparable to that of privately insured individuals and better than that of uninsured individuals, but may have greater health care needs and greater difficulty accessing specialty and dental care.
- **Transparency and oversight**: The lack of complete and reliable data on states' spending—including provider payments and state financing of the non-federal share of Medicaid—hinders federal oversight, and GAO has recommended steps to improve the data on and scrutiny of states' spending. Also, improvements in the Department of Health and Human Services' (HHS) criteria, policy, and process for approving states' spending on demonstrations—state projects that may test new ways to deliver or pay for care—are needed to potentially prevent billions of dollars in unnecessary federal spending, as GAO previously recommended.
- **Program integrity**: The program's size and diversity make it vulnerable to improper payments. Improper payments, such as payments for non-covered services, totaled an estimated $17.5 billion in fiscal year 2014, according to HHS. An effective federal-state partnership is key to ensuring the most appropriate use of funds by, among other things, (1) setting appropriate payment rates for managed care organizations, and (2) ensuring only eligible individuals and providers participate in Medicaid.

Medicaid: Key Issues Facing the Program 3

- **Federal financing approach**: Automatic federal assistance during economic downturns and more equitable federal allocations of Medicaid funds to states (by better accounting for states' ability to fund Medicaid) could better align federal funding with states' needs, offering states greater fiscal stability. GAO has suggested that Congress could consider enacting a funding formula that provides automatic, timely, and temporary increased assistance in response to national economic downturns.

Medicaid's ongoing transformation—due to the Patient Protection and Affordable Care Act (PPACA), the aging of the U.S. population, and other changes to state programs—highlights the importance of federal oversight, given the implications for enrollees and program costs. Attention to Medicaid's transformation and the key issues facing the program will be important to ensuring that Medicaid is both effective for the enrollees who rely on it and accountable to the taxpayers. GAO has multiple ongoing studies in these areas and will continue to monitor the Medicaid program for the Congress.

ABBREVIATIONS

EPOP	employment-to-population ratio
CBO	Congressional Budget Office
CHIP	State Children's Health Insurance Program
CMS	Centers for Medicare & Medicaid Services
DSH	disproportionate share hospital
EPSDT	Early and Periodic Screening, Diagnostic, and Treatment
FMAP	Federal Medical Assistance Percentage
FPL	federal poverty level
HCERA	Health Care and Education Reconciliation Act of 2010
HHS	Department of Health and Human Services
IT	information technology
LTSS	long-term services and supports
MACPAC	Medicaid and CHIP Payment and Access Commission
MCO	managed care organization
MMIS	Medicaid Management Information System
MSIS	Medicaid Statistical Information System
T-MSIS	Transformed Medicaid Statistical Information System

OIG	Office of Inspector General
PECOS	Provider Enrollment, Chain, and Ownership System
PPACA	Patient Protection and Affordable Care Act
UPL	upper payment limit

* * *

July 30, 2015

Congressional Addressees

The Medicaid program marks its 50th anniversary on July 30, 2015. Over the past half-century, Medicaid has grown to be one of the largest sources of health care coverage and financing for a diverse low-income and medically needy population. It is the nation's second largest health care program as measured by expenditures, behind only Medicare. Medicaid is also a significant component of federal and state budgets, with estimated outlays of $529 billion in fiscal year 2015, of which $320 billion is expected to be financed by the federal government and $209 billion by the states.[1] Medicaid was estimated to account for the second largest share of state spending that year, exceeded only by state spending on elementary and secondary education. An important health care safety net, Medicaid covered about 72 million individuals—roughly one-fifth of the U.S. population—during fiscal year 2013.[2] Medicaid's diverse enrollee population includes children, low-income adults, individuals who are elderly, and those who are disabled. The program covers a comprehensive set of services, including physician, and inpatient and outpatient hospital care, and is also a particularly significant source of health care coverage and financing for certain services. For example, Medicaid is the nation's primary payer of long-term services and supports (LTSS), including nursing home care and home- and community-based services to allow individuals to age in their homes.

An already large and complex program, Medicaid is undergoing a period of transformative change, as enrollment is growing under the Patient Protection and Affordable Care Act (PPACA), and Medicaid spending is projected to increase by nearly 60 percent by fiscal year 2023.[3] For example, PPACA permitted states to expand their Medicaid programs by covering certain low-income adults not historically eligible for Medicaid coverage, and more than half of the states have done so. Further, among other factors, the aging of the population and new developments with technology are both transforming and challenging Medicaid and the rest of the U.S. health care system. In addition, changing economic conditions have influenced the number and mix of individuals who are eligible for Medicaid coverage, and will continue to do so in the future.

Medicaid is designed as a federal-state partnership, and both the federal government and the states play important roles in ensuring that Medicaid is fiscally sustainable over time and effective in meeting the needs of the vulnerable populations it serves. Medicaid is financed jointly by the federal government and states, administered at the state level, and overseen at the federal level by the Centers for Medicare & Medicaid Services (CMS), within the Department of Health and Human Services (HHS). Medicaid, by design, allows significant flexibility for states to design and implement their programs. This has influenced the development of the program and has resulted in over 50 distinct state- based programs that vary in how health care is delivered, financed, reimbursed, and overseen. While state flexibility is a key element of the program, federal oversight is important to help ensure that funds are used appropriately and that enrollees can access quality care. However, the size, growth, and diversity of the Medicaid program create significant challenges for oversight. There is an inherent tension between states' efforts to design programs that best meet their local needs and federal efforts to oversee the states' programs. Attention to the issues facing Medicaid and the effectiveness of its federal-state partnership will be important for ensuring that Medicaid is both effective for the enrollees who rely on it and accountable to the taxpayers.

We have reported over the years on a number of challenges facing Medicaid, as well as on gaps in federal oversight of the program.[4] In this report, we describe (1) key issues that face the Medicaid program, based on our work; and (2) how the high risk nature of Medicaid—and this period of transformative change in the program—have implications for federal oversight. We prepared this report under the authority of the Comptroller General to conduct work at GAO's initiative to assist Congress with its oversight responsibilities.

To conduct this work, we reviewed reports on Medicaid that we issued from January 2005—10 years from when we began this review—through July 2015, including our most recent high risk update, and identified key issues facing the program and factors that have implications for federal oversight. We also reviewed documentation from CMS and interviewed CMS officials about the status of our prior recommendations, as well as current CMS efforts related to Medicaid. The issues we discuss are neither inclusive of all the issues facing Medicaid nor all the issues CMS faces in its oversight efforts. For a list of related reports, see "Related GAO Products" at the end of this report. Please see the scope and methodology for each of these reports for details on how we conducted that work. In addition, appendix I lists open matters for congressional consideration and selected open GAO recommendations regarding Medicaid, as of July 2015. (GAO has made more than 80 recommendations regarding Medicaid since January 2005.)

We conducted this performance audit from January 2015 to July 2015 in accordance with generally accepted government auditing standards. Those standards require that we plan and perform the audit to obtain sufficient, appropriate evidence to provide a reasonable basis for our findings and conclusions based on our audit objectives. We believe that the evidence obtained provides a reasonable basis for our findings and conclusions based on our audit objectives.

RESULTS IN BRIEF

As the Medicaid program marks its 50th year, it faces a range of key issues, as indicated by our prior work. (See figure 1.) Attention to these key issues—access to quality care; transparency and oversight; program integrity; and federal financing—will be important to ensuring that the Medicaid program is both effective for the enrollees who rely on it and accountable to the taxpayers.

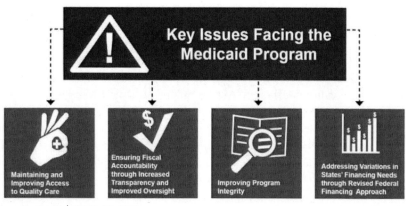

Source: GAO. | GAO-15-677

Figure 1. Key Issues Facing the Medicaid Program.

- First, maintaining and improving access to quality care is critical to ensuring that the program is effective for the individuals who rely on it. Although Medicaid enrollees report having access to care that is generally comparable to that of privately insured individuals, some enrollees may face challenges, such as in obtaining specialty care (like mental health care) or dental care. CMS has taken steps to help ensure enrollees' access to care and we have recommended additional steps that could bolster those efforts. We recommended in September 2009, for example, that CMS ensure that states with inadequate managed care dental provider networks take action to strengthen those networks. CMS has reported taking steps to improve these networks, but we believe more can be done in this area. CMS also has ongoing efforts to collect data from states to help assess Medicaid enrollees' access to care, and in April 2011 we recommended CMS take steps to improve its data. For example, we recommended that CMS work with states to explore options for reporting on the receipt of services separately for children in managed care and fee-for-service delivery models. CMS officials indicated that they do not plan to require states to report such information, but we continue to believe this information is important for monitoring and ensuring access to care.

- Second, efforts to ensure fiscal accountability through increased transparency and improved oversight can help make certain that Medicaid funds are used appropriately. A lack of reliable CMS data about program payments to providers and state financing of the non-federal share of Medicaid hinders oversight, and our work has pointed to the need for better data, as well as improved policy and oversight. In addition, gaps in HHS's criteria, process, and policy for approving states' spending on demonstrations—state projects that test new ways to deliver Medicaid benefits—raises questions about billions of dollars in federal spending. Improvements are needed to ensure that demonstrations do not increase federal Medicaid spending, and that demonstrations further Medicaid objectives. HHS and CMS have taken important steps in recent years to improve transparency, oversight, and fiscal accountability, and we have recommended additional steps that would build on those efforts. For example, in April 2015, we recommended that CMS take steps to ensure that states report accurate provider-specific payment data and develop a policy and process for reviewing payments to individual providers to determine whether they are economical and efficient, and HHS concurred with our recommendations.

- Third, improving program integrity can help ensure the most appropriate use of Medicaid funds. The program's size and diversity make it particularly vulnerable to improper payments, including payments made for treatments or services that were not covered by the program, that were not medically necessary, or that were billed for but never provided. Improper payments are a significant cost to Medicaid—totaling an estimated $17.5 billion in fiscal year 2014, according to HHS. An effective federal-state partnership is key to ensuring the most appropriate use of funds by (1) identifying and preventing improper payments in both fee-for-service and managed care, (2) setting appropriate payment rates for managed care organizations, and (3) ensuring only eligible individuals and providers participate in Medicaid. CMS has taken steps to improve program integrity, and we have recommended other steps that would bolster those efforts. In May 2014, for example, we recommended CMS take steps to improve oversight of growing Medicaid managed care expenditures; CMS has taken some steps and we believe even more can be done in this area.
- Fourth, Medicaid's federal-state partnership could be improved through a revised federal financing approach that better addresses variations in states' financing needs. The federal government currently pays a share of Medicaid expenditures according to a statutory formula based on each state's per capita income relative to the national average. Automatically providing increased federal financial assistance to states affected by national economic downturns—through temporary changes to the federal funding formula—could help provide timely and targeted assistance that is more responsive to states' economic conditions than past federal assistance when Congress acted to temporarily increase support to states by increasing the share of Medicaid expenditures paid by the federal government. We suggested in November 2011 that Congress could consider enacting a federal funding formula that provides such automatic, targeted and timely assistance. In addition, we have described revisions to the current federal funding formula that could more equitably allocate Medicaid funds to states by better accounting for their ability to fund Medicaid. These improvements could better align federal funding with each state's resources, demand for services,

and costs; better facilitate state budget planning; and provide states with greater fiscal stability during times of economic stress.

Medicaid's size, complexity, oversight challenges, and ongoing transformation highlight the importance of federal monitoring. In 2003, GAO designated Medicaid as a high-risk program due to its size, growth, diversity of programs, and concerns about gaps in oversight—and more than a decade later, those factors remain. In addition, the effects of changes brought on by PPACA, as well as the aging of the U.S. population, will continue to emerge in the coming years and are likely to exacerbate the challenges in federal oversight. Other changes in state programs, such as changes to health care delivery and payment approaches, will continue to pose challenges to federal oversight. These changes have implications for enrollees and for program costs, and underscore the importance of ongoing attention to federal oversight efforts. We have multiple ongoing studies on Medicaid's transformation and the issues facing the program, and will continue to monitor the Medicaid program for the Congress.

HHS reviewed a draft of this report and provided technical comments, which we incorporated as appropriate.

BACKGROUND

Medicaid finances the delivery of health care services for a diverse low-income and medically needy population. The Social Security Act, which Congress amended in 1965 to establish the Medicaid program, provides the statutory framework for the program, setting broad parameters for states that choose to participate and implement their own Medicaid programs. CMS is responsible for overseeing state Medicaid programs to ensure compliance with federal requirements.

Medicaid Eligibility, Enrollment, Services, and Expenditures

Historically, Medicaid eligibility has been limited to certain categories of low-income individuals—such as children, parents, pregnant women, persons with disabilities, and individuals age 65 and older.[5] In addition to these historical eligibility standards, PPACA permitted states to expand their Medicaid programs by covering non-elderly, non-pregnant adults with incomes at or below 133 percent of the federal poverty level (FPL).[6] As of May 2015, 29 states, including the District of Columbia, had expanded their Medicaid programs to cover this new adult group, and one other state's proposed expansion was pending federal approval.

Federal law requires state Medicaid programs to cover a wide array of mandatory services, and permits states to cover additional services at their option.[7] Consequently, Medicaid generally covers a wide range of health care services that can be categorized into broad types of coverage, including hospital care; non-hospital acute care, such as physician, dental, laboratory, and preventive services; prescription drugs; and LTSS in institutions and in the community.[8] (See figure 2 for an overview of Medicaid expenditures by category.)

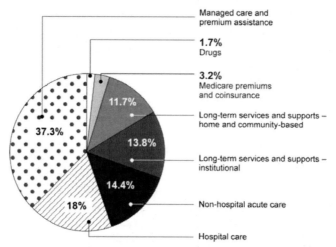

Source: GAO analysis of Medicaid and CHIP Payment and Access Commission (MACPAC) data. | GAO-15-677

Notes: Data are based on MACPAC analysis of CMS-64 data and include both federal and state funds for the 50 states and the District of Columbia, but exclude expenditures for administration. Medicaid benefit spending figures include federal and state spending for 2014 as of February 25, 2015, and were subject to change if states revised their expenditure data. The figures for long-term services and supports, drugs, non-hospital acute care, and hospital care only include Medicaid expenditures for services that are provided through fee-for-service; additional spending on these services may be included in the "Managed care and premium assistance" category. Managed care payments can affect the distribution of spending across categories because they are not made for specific services. Data do not add to 100 due to rounding.

"Managed care and premium assistance" includes payments for comprehensive and limited-benefit managed care plans, primary care case management, employer-sponsored premium assistance, and other payments.

"Drugs" includes spending on drugs net of rebates received from drug manufacturers.

"Long-term services and supports – home and community-based" includes home health, personal care, and other services.

"Long-term services and supports – institutional" includes the services of nursing facilities, intermediate care facilities for persons with intellectual disabilities, and mental health facilities.

"Non-hospital acute care" includes services of physicians, dentists, and other practitioners; labs and X-rays; hospice; physical, occupational, speech, hearing, or language therapy; rehabilitative services; diagnostic screening and preventive services; and other services.

"Hospital care" includes inpatient and outpatient hospital services; disproportionate share hospital payments; emergency services; and payments to critical access hospitals.

Figure 2. Medicaid Expenditures by Category, Fiscal Year 2014.

In recent years, we and others have examined patterns of service utilization and expenditures within the Medicaid population and found that enrollment and expenditures vary among the different categories of enrollees. For example, for fiscal year 2011, children constituted the largest category of enrollees (47.4 percent), but accounted for a small share of Medicaid expenditures (19 percent). In that same year, enrollees with disabilities (14.7 percent of Medicaid enrollees) accounted for the largest share of Medicaid expenditures (42.7 percent). (See figure 3.) In addition, we found that, generally, a small subset of Medicaid enrollees— such as those with institutional care needs or chronic conditions—account for a large portion of Medicaid expenditures.[9]

Health Care Delivery Models

States have traditionally provided Medicaid benefits using a fee-for-service system, where health care providers are paid for each service delivered. However, according to CMS, in the past 15 years, states have increasingly implemented managed care systems for delivering Medicaid services. In a managed care delivery system, enrollees obtain some portion of their Medicaid services from a managed care organization (MCO) under contract with the state, and capitation payments to MCOs are typically made on a predetermined, per person per month basis. Nationally, about 37 percent of Medicaid spending in fiscal year 2014 was attributable to Medicaid managed care. Many states are expanding their use of managed care to additional geographic areas and Medicaid populations. States oversee Medicaid MCOs through contracts and reporting requirements.

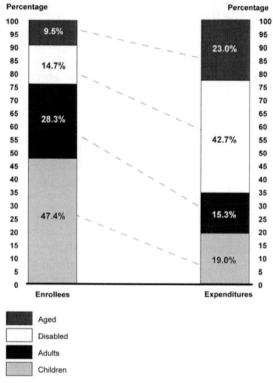

Source: GAO analysis of Medicaid and CHIP Payment and Access Commission (MACPAC) data. | GAO-15-677

Note: Enrollees include individuals in 50 states and the District of Columbia ever enrolled in Medicaid during fiscal year 2011. Expenditures include both federal and state funds for 48 states and the District of Columbia, but exclude spending for administration and Disproportionate Share Hospital payments. Due to anomalies in the expenditure data, MACPAC excluded Maine and Tennessee from the expenditure data.

Figure 3. Medicaid Enrollment and Expenditures, by Eligibility Group, Fiscal Year 2011.

Medicaid: Key Issues Facing the Program

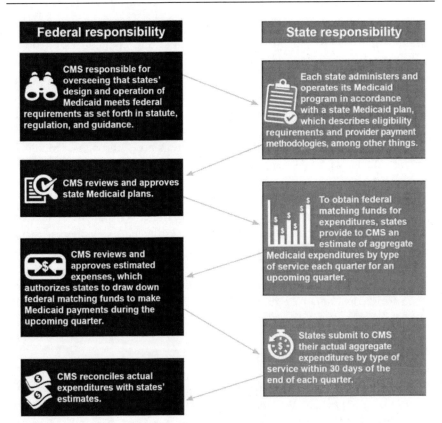

Source: GAO. | GAO-15-677

Note: If a state wishes to make amendments to its state Medicaid plan, it must seek approval from the Centers for Medicare & Medicaid Services (CMS). Similarly, a state that desires to change its Medicaid program in ways that deviate from certain federal requirements may seek to do so through a Medicaid demonstration, outside of its state Medicaid plan. States must submit an application describing the proposed demonstration to the Department of Health and Human Services (HHS) for review. HHS will specify the special terms and conditions that encompass the requirements for an approved demonstration.

Figure 4. Federal-State Medicaid Partnership Framework.

The Federal-State Partnership

CMS provides oversight and technical assistance for the Medicaid program, but states are primarily responsible for administering their respective

Medicaid programs' day-to-day operations—including determining eligibility, enrolling individuals and providers, and adjudicating claims—within broad federal requirements. Each state has a Medicaid state plan that describes how the state will administer its Medicaid program consistent with federal requirements. States submit these state plans for approval to CMS, but have significant flexibility to structure their programs to best suit their needs. In addition, within certain parameters, states may innovate outside of many of Medicaid's otherwise applicable requirements through Medicaid demonstrations, with HHS approval.[10] For example, states may test ways to obtain savings or efficiencies in how services are delivered in order to cover otherwise ineligible services or populations.

CMS makes quarterly grant awards to states to cover the federal share of Medicaid expenditures based on each state's estimated expenditures. States draw down these funds on a real time basis to make program payments. Subsequently, states submit their actual quarterly expenditures, and CMS reviews these and reconciles them with the estimated expenditures.[11] (See figure 4 for a diagram of the federal-state Medicaid partnership framework.)

Financing the Medicaid Program

The federal government matches state Medicaid expenditures based on a statutory formula—the Federal Medical Assistance Percentage (FMAP). Under the FMAP, the federal government pays a share of Medicaid expenditures based on each state's per capita income (PCI) relative to the national average. The formula is designed such that the federal government pays a larger portion of Medicaid costs in states with lower per capita incomes relative to the national average. A state's regular FMAP is calculated using the following formula:

$$\text{State FMAP} = 1.00 - 0.45 \, (\text{State PCI} \, / \, \text{U.S. PCI})^2$$

Federal law specifies that the regular FMAP will be no lower than 50 percent and no higher than 83 percent. For fiscal year 2015, regular FMAP rates ranged from 50.00 percent to 73.58 percent.

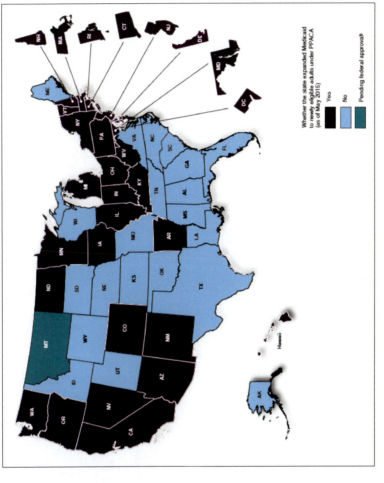

(See Appendix II for additional information on Figure 5).

Sources: GAO based on information from the Medicaid and CHIP Payment and Access Commission (MACPAC) (enrollment and spending data); Office of the Assistant Secretary for Planning and Evaluation, Department of Health and Human Services (regular FMAPs); and The Henry J. Kaiser Family Foundation (Medicaid expansion status) (data); Map Resources (map). | GAO-15-677

[a] Medicaid enrollment figures reflect full-year equivalent enrollment, which is the sum of monthly enrollment totals, divided by 12.

[b] Medicaid benefit spending figures include federal and state spending for 2014 as of Feb. 25, 2015, and were subject to change if states revised their expenditure data.

[c] The federal government matches state Medicaid expenditures based on a statutory formula—the FMAP. The regular FMAP differs from the FMAP that may apply to certain individuals, such as those newly eligible for Medicaid under PPACA.

[d] Comprehensive risk-based managed care plans do not include limited-benefit plans or primary care case management programs.

[e] State had a change in total enrollment of 10 percent or more over the prior year, which may reflect data anomalies and may be updated in the future.

[f] MACPAC did not report managed care information for Maine, Tennessee, or Vermont due to data anomalies.

[g] State enacted legislation expanding Medicaid; federal approval of the expansion is required before it can be implemented.

Figure 5. Regular Federal Medical Assistance Percentage (FMAP); Medicaid Enrollment, Spending, and Managed Care; and Medicaid Expansion under the Patient Protection and Affordable Care Act (PPACA), by State.

Under PPACA, state Medicaid expenditures for certain Medicaid enrollees, newly eligible under the statute, are subject to a higher federal match. States that choose to expand their Medicaid programs receive an FMAP of 100 percent beginning in 2014 for expenditures for the PPACA-expansion enrollees—those who were not previously eligible for Medicaid and are eligible now under PPACA's expansion of eligibility criteria. The FMAP is to gradually diminish to 90 percent by 2020. States also receive an FMAP above the state's regular match (but below the PPACA- expansion FMAP) for their Medicaid expenditures for the state-expansion enrollees—those who would not have been eligible for Medicaid prior to PPACA except that they were covered under a state's pre-PPACA "expansion" of eligibility through, for example, a Medicaid demonstration.[12] This FMAP is to gradually increase and eventually equal the FMAP for the PPACA-expansion enrollees beginning in 2019. The formula used to calculate the state-expansion FMAP rates is based on a state's regular FMAP rate so the enhanced FMAP rate will vary from state to state until 2019.

See figure 5 for the variation across states in the regular FMAP; Medicaid spending, enrollment, and managed care enrollment; and whether the state had expanded Medicaid coverage to newly eligible adults under PPACA as of May 2015. See appendix II for the information in tabular form.

KEY ISSUES FACING THE MEDICAID PROGRAM

Maintaining and Improving Access to Quality Care

Medicaid enrollees report access to medical care that is generally comparable to that of privately insured individuals. However, some enrollees may face access challenges, such as in obtaining specialty care or dental care. CMS has taken steps to help ensure enrollees' access to care and additional steps could bolster those efforts. CMS also has ongoing efforts to collect data from states to help assess Medicaid enrollees' access to care, but better data are needed.

Medicaid Enrollees Report Access to Care that is Generally Comparable to the Privately Insured, but Some Face Particular Access Challenges

We have found that Medicaid enrollees report experiencing access to medical care that is generally comparable to that of privately insured individuals. For example, according to national survey data, few enrollees covered by Medicaid for a full year—less than 4 percent—reported difficulty obtaining necessary medical care or prescription medicine in 2008 and 2009, similar to privately insured individuals.[13] (See figure 6.) Regarding children, respondents with children covered by Medicaid reported positive responses to most questions about their ability to obtain care, and at levels generally comparable to those with private insurance, from 2007 through 2010.[14]

- Medicaid enrollees report access to care that is generally comparable to the privately insured, but some face particular access challenges.
- Better data needed to help assess and improve Medicaid enrollees' access to care.

Source: GAO. | GAO-15-677

Although few Medicaid enrollees report difficulty obtaining necessary care in general, our work indicates that particular populations can face particular challenges obtaining care. For example, about 7.8 percent of working-age adults with full-year Medicaid reported difficulty obtaining care compared with 3.3 percent of similar adults with private insurance— a statistically significant difference. Some enrollees face particular challenges, such as accessing services. For example, Medicaid enrollees were more likely than individuals with private insurance to report factors such as lack of transportation and long wait times as reasons for delaying medical care.[15] (See figure 7.) We have also found that Medicaid-covered adults may be more likely to have certain health conditions that can be identified and managed through preventive services, such as obesity and diabetes, than individuals with private insurance. However, states' Medicaid coverage of certain preventive services for adults has varied, which has resulted in different levels of coverage across states.[16]

Medicaid: Key Issues Facing the Program

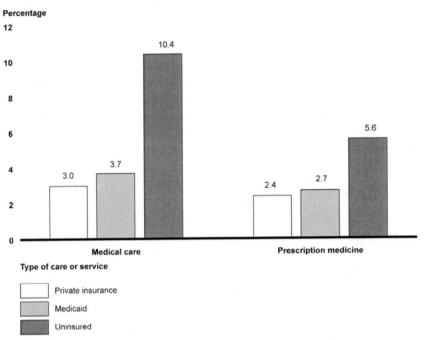

Source: GAO analysis of Medical Expenditure Panel Survey data. | GAO-15-677
Note: This figure includes only those individuals who reported coverage or lack of coverage for the entire year (2008 or 2009, or both). These Medicaid data include children enrolled in the State Children's Health Insurance Program.

Figure 6. Percentage of Medicaid-Covered Individuals Who Reported Difficulties Obtaining Necessary Care or Services, by Full-Year Insurance Status, Calendar Years 2008-2009.

Specialty care, such as mental health care and dental care, may be particularly difficult for some Medicaid enrollees to obtain.

Access to Specialty Care, Including Mental Health Care

National surveys of enrollees and our own surveys of state Medicaid officials and physicians have consistently indicated that Medicaid enrollees may have difficulty obtaining specialty care, such as mental health care. In our survey of state Medicaid officials in 2012,[17] for example, officials in about half of the states reported challenges ensuring enough participating specialty providers for Medicaid enrollees, such as in obstetrics and gynecology, surgical specialties, and pediatric services. In addition, we found that about 21 percent of respondents with Medicaid-covered children reported that it was only sometimes or never easy to see a specialist, compared to about 13 percent of respondents with privately insured children, from 2008 through 2010.[18] Our 2010 national survey of physicians found that specialty physicians were generally more willing to accept privately insured children as new patients than Medicaid-covered children; similarly, more physicians reported having difficulty referring Medicaid-covered children to specialty providers than reported having difficulty referring privately insured children.[19] (See figure 8.)

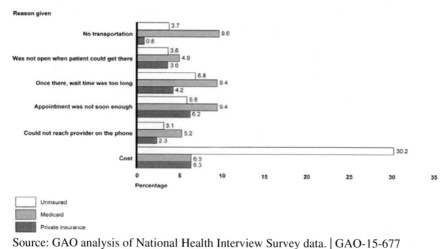

Source: GAO analysis of National Health Interview Survey data. | GAO-15-677
Note: This figure reflects individuals who reported their insurance status at the time the survey was administered. There was not a statistically significant difference between individuals with Medicaid and private insurance citing cost as a reason for delayed medical care, or reporting that a provider was not open when he or she could get there.

Figure 7. Percentage of Individuals Who Cited Specific Reasons for Delaying Medical Care in Calendar Year 2009, by Insurance Status.

We have also found that both Medicaid-covered adults and children may face challenges obtaining mental health care. Research has shown that Medicaid enrollees experience a higher rate of mental health conditions than those with private insurance.[20] Officials we interviewed from six states that expanded Medicaid under PPACA generally reported that Medicaid expansion had increased the availability of mental health treatment for newly eligible adults, but cited access concerns for new Medicaid enrollees due to shortages of Medicaid-participating psychiatrists and psychiatric drug prescribers.[21] In our 2012 national survey, state officials reported problems ensuring sufficient psychiatry providers for Medicaid enrollees.[22] Among Medicaid-covered children, national survey data from 2007 through 2009 indicated that 14 percent of noninstitutionalized Medicaid-covered children had a potential need for mental health services, but most of these children did not receive mental health services.[23] In addition, many Medicaid-covered children who took psychotropic medications (medications that affect mood, thought, or behavior) did not receive other mental health services during the same year.[24]

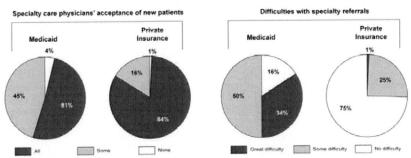

Source: GAO. | GAO-15-677
Notes: Participating physicians are those enrolled as Medicaid and State Children's Health Insurance Program (CHIP) providers. Our survey asked physicians about both Medicaid- and CHIP-covered children, and in reporting our results we did not report separate information for these two populations. For the purposes of this report, we refer to these survey findings as applying to Medicaid-covered children, who account for the majority of all children who are covered by either program. Numbers may not sum to 100 percent because of rounding.

Figure 8. Specialty Physicians' Acceptance of Children as New Patients, and Physicians' Level of Difficulty Referring Children for Specialty Care (among Physicians Participating in Medicaid), 2010.

HHS and CMS have taken steps to improve Medicaid enrollees' access to quality mental health services. CMS has, for example, provided guidance to states about resources available to meet the needs of children with mental health problems. In addition, HHS has issued guidance and provided technical assistance for states regarding oversight of psychotropic medication prescribing for children in foster care.[25] Because HHS's guidance does not specifically address oversight of foster children receiving medications through managed care organizations, we recommended in 2014 that HHS issue additional guidance about oversight of prescribing medications for those children. HHS agreed with our recommendation in comments on our draft report.[26] In May 2015, CMS indicated that it no longer agreed that additional guidance was necessary, stating that its existing guidance applied to managed care settings. We continue to believe that our recommendation is valid. We found that many states were, or were transitioning to, managed care organizations to administer prescription-drug benefits, and that selected states had taken only limited steps to plan for the oversight of drug prescribing for foster children receiving care through these organizations—creating a risk that controls instituted under fee-for-service may not remain once states move to managed care. As we reported, additional HHS guidance that helps states prepare and implement monitoring efforts within the context of a managed-care environment could help ensure appropriate oversight of psychotropic medications to children in foster care.

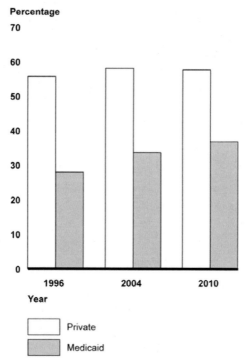

Source: GAO analysis of Medical Expenditure Panel Survey data. | GAO-15-677
Notes: For 2004 and 2010, Medicaid includes children enrolled in the State Children's Health Insurance Program.

Figure 9. Percentage of Children, Ages 0-20 Years, with Private and Medicaid Dental Coverage with a Dental Visit, 1996, 2004, and 2010.

Access to Dental Care

In recent years, Medicaid enrollees' use of dental services increased, but some access problems persist. We found that while the percentage of individuals with Medicaid dental coverage who had a dental visit increased from 28 percent in 1996 to 34 percent in 2010, individuals with Medicaid dental coverage were still much less likely than privately insured individuals to have visited the dentist. About two-thirds of Medicaid- covered children, for example, did not visit the dentist at all in 2010, while most privately insured children did.[27] (See figure 9.) This difference in use of dental services persisted despite the fact that Medicaid-covered children may have a greater need for dental care than privately insured children. We have found that Medicaid-covered children are almost twice as likely to have untreated tooth decay as privately insured children.[28] In addition, states have found it particularly challenging to ensure a sufficient number of dental providers for Medicaid enrollees.[29]

CMS has taken some steps to address access to dental care, and other steps could build on those efforts. In 2010, for example, the agency launched a Children's Oral Health Initiative that aimed to, among other things, increase the proportion of Medicaid and State Children's Health Insurance Program (CHIP) children who receive a preventive dental service. In response to our prior recommendations, CMS also took steps to ensure that states gather information on the provision of Medicaid dental services by managed care programs, and to improve the accuracy of the data on HHS's Insure Kids Now website, which provides state- reported information on dentists who serve children enrolled in Medicaid and CHIP.[30] We recommended that CMS require states to verify that dentists listed on the Insure Kids Now website have not been excluded from Medicaid by HHS, and periodically verify that excluded providers are not included on the lists of dentists posted by the states.[31] However, CMS has said that it relies on states to provide accurate lists of eligible dentists and that data issues prevent the agency from independently verifying that excluded providers are not included on the website.[32] We continue to believe that CMS should require states to ensure that excluded providers are not listed on the website, so that it does not present inaccurate information about providers available to serve Medicaid-covered children. We also recommended that for states that provide Medicaid dental services through managed care organizations, CMS ensure that states with inadequate managed care dental provider networks take action to strengthen these networks.[33] CMS has reported taking steps to improve these networks, including meeting with national dental associations, but we believe more can

24 United States Government Accountability Office

be done to identify inadequate networks and, once inadequate networks are identified, to work with states to strengthen them to help ensure that they meet the needs of Medicaid enrollees.

Better Data Needed to Help Assess and Improve Medicaid Enrollees' Access to Care

CMS has ongoing efforts to collect data from states to help assess Medicaid enrollees' access to care and identify areas for improvement. States are required to submit certain types of data to CMS, and they can opt to submit other types of data. For example, states are required to submit reports on the provision of certain services for eligible children, as part of the Early and Periodic Screening, Diagnostic, and Treatment (EPSDT) benefit.[34] These reports, known as CMS 416 reports, include such information as the number of children receiving well-child checkups and the number of children referred for treatment services for conditions identified during well-child checkups. CMS has used these reports to identify states with low reported rates of service provision, to help identify state Medicaid programs needing improvements.[35] In addition, states voluntarily report Child Core Set measures, which assess the quality of care provided through Medicaid and CHIP, and include, for example, measures of access to primary care and the receipt of follow-up care for children prescribed attention deficit hyperactivity disorder medication. Also, states that use managed care plans to deliver services for Medicaid and CHIP enrollees are required to annually review these plans to evaluate the quality, timeliness, and access to services that the plans provide—and submit their "external quality review" reports to CMS.[36]

In 2011, we reported on problems and gaps in the required CMS 416 reports. We found that states sometimes made reporting errors, and in some cases those errors overstated the extent to which children received well-child checkups.[37] In addition, states did not always report required data on how many Medicaid-covered children were referred for additional services to address conditions identified through check-ups. Finally, we found that CMS did not require states to report information on whether Medicaid-covered children actually received services for which they were referred—or to report information separately for children in managed care versus those in fee-for-service systems.

CMS has since taken steps to improve the CMS 416 data, and we believe more can be done, as discussed below.

Medicaid: Key Issues Facing the Program   25

- In response to our recommendation that CMS establish a plan to review the accuracy and completeness of the CMS 416 data and ensure that problems are corrected, CMS has established an automated quality assurance process to identify obvious reporting errors and as of March 2015 was developing training for state staff responsible for the data.

- We also recommended that CMS work with states to explore options for capturing information on children's receipt of services for which they were referred. The agency has issued guidance to states about how to report referrals for health care services, but has not required states to report whether children receive services for which they are referred. CMS officials noted that data collection tools other than the CMS 416 reports, such as the Child Core Set measures, provide CMS with information on whether children are receiving needed care—and that HHS was developing additional measures to help fill gaps in assessing children's care. While these are positive steps, we have noted that CMS's ability to monitor children's access to services is dependent on consistent, reliable, complete, and sufficiently detailed data from each state.[38] The Child Core Set measures, for example, are voluntarily reported by states, and we have reported that although the number of states reporting measures has increased in recent years, that states have varied considerably in the number of measures they reported.[39] We continue to believe that information on whether children receive services for which they are referred is important for monitoring and ensuring their access to care.

- We also recommended that CMS work with states to explore options for reporting on the receipt of services separately for children in managed care and fee-for-service delivery models. However, CMS officials indicated that they do not plan to require states to report such information, in part, to limit the reporting burden for states. CMS officials added that the states report information on children's access to care through their managed care external quality review reports. While this is a positive step, these reports do not represent a consistent set of measures used by all states that CMS can use for oversight purposes. We continue to believe that having accurate and complete information on children's access to health services, by delivery model, is an important element of monitoring and ensuring access to care and that CMS should fully implement this recommendation.

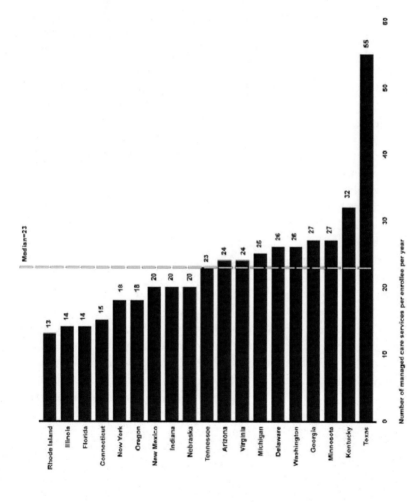

Source: GAO analysis of Medicaid data. | GAO-15-677

Note: Enrollees included in our analysis were eligible to receive full Medicaid benefits and were enrolled in a comprehensive managed care plan in at least one month during calendar year 2010. We excluded enrollees who were enrolled in a comprehensive managed care plan if during the calendar year of our analysis they had other sources of health coverage in addition to Medicaid. We focused our analysis on professional services and excluded dental and behavioral health services and any services paid on a fee-for-service basis.

Figure 10. Adult Professional Service Utilization in Selected States, 2010.

Our 2015 report on managed care services used by Medicaid enrollees in 19 states highlighted the importance of having reliable data to help understand patterns of managed care utilization and the impact that managed care delivery models may have on enrollees' access to care.[40] We found that the number of managed care services used by adult and child enrollees varied by state, population, type of service, and whether enrollees were enrolled in comprehensive managed care plans for all or part of the year. For example, the number of services per enrollee per year for adults ranged from about 13 to 55 services per enrollee per year, across the 19 states.[41] (See figure 10.) With regard to children, in almost every selected state, the total service utilization was higher for children who were enrolled in comprehensive managed care for less than the full year, when compared with those enrolled for a full year. This type of information can be useful for understanding access to care among enrollees in Medicaid managed care plans. A detailed, interactive display of the data used to support our findings is available at http://www.gao.gov/products/GAO-15-481.

- Data limitations hinder oversight.
- Improving HHS's review and approval process for demonstration spending may prevent unnecessary federal spending.

Source: GAO. | GAO-15-677

Ensuring Fiscal Accountability through Increased Transparency and Improved Oversight

Given Medicaid's size, complexity, and diversity, transparency in how funds are used is critical to ensuring fiscal accountability. However, a lack of reliable CMS data about program payments and state financing of the non-federal share of Medicaid hinders oversight, and our work has pointed to the need for better data, as well as improved policy and oversight, to ensure that funds are being used appropriately and efficiently. In addition, gaps in HHS's criteria, process, and policy for approving states' demonstration spending raise questions about billions of dollars in federal spending. While HHS and CMS have taken important steps in recent years to improve transparency, oversight, and fiscal accountability, more can be done to build on those efforts.

Data Limitations Hinder Oversight

Data limitations hinder the transparency of program payments and state financing sources, and hinder federal oversight.

Federal Data on Program Payments

CMS does not have the complete and reliable data needed to understand the payments states make to individual providers, nor does it have a transparent policy and standard process for assessing whether those payments are appropriate. States have considerable flexibility in setting payment rates that providers, such as hospitals, receive for services rendered to individual Medicaid enrollees. In addition to these regular claims-based payments, states may make (and obtain federal matching funds for) payments to certain providers that are not specifically linked to services Medicaid enrollees receive. These payments can help offset any remaining costs of care for Medicaid patients,[42] and in some cases can be used to offset costs incurred treating uninsured patients. These types of payments are known as supplemental payments, which include disproportionate share hospital (DSH) payments and other payments, such as those known as Medicaid upper payment limit (UPL) supplemental payments.[43] States have some flexibility in how they distribute supplemental payments to individual providers. However, Medicaid payments to providers should not be excessive, as the law states that they must be "economical and efficient."[44]

We have had longstanding concerns about federal oversight of supplemental payments, which our work has found to be a significant and growing component of Medicaid spending, totaling at least $43 billion in fiscal year 2011.[45] CMS oversight of provider supplemental payments is limited because the agency does not require states to report provider- specific data on these payments, nor does it have a policy and standard process for determining whether Medicaid payments to individual providers are economical and efficient. States may have incentives to make excessive Medicaid payments to certain institutional providers, such as local government hospitals needing or receiving financial support from the state. Absent a process to review these payments—and absent data on total payments individual providers receive—the agency may not identify potentially excessive payments to providers, and the federal government could be paying states hundreds of millions—or billions—of dollars more than what is appropriate, as shown in the examples below.[46]

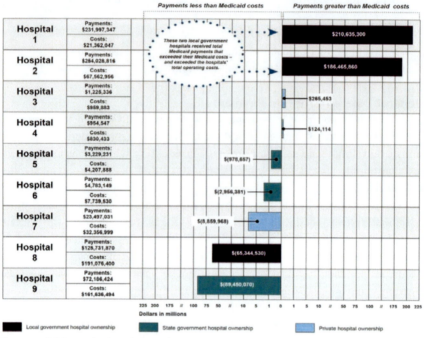

Source: GAO analysis of data from Centers for Medicare & Medicaid Services (inpatient hospital claims) and New York (hospital ownership, supplemental payments, and Medicaid Cost Reports). | GAO-15-677

Notes: These hospitals were selected based on having the highest daily payments for regular payments that were adjusted to account for differences in the conditions of the patients treated at the hospitals, commonly referred to as "case-mix" adjustment, and upper payment limit (UPL) supplemental payments in each provider ownership group—local government, state government, and private. We selected a total of nine hospitals—three local government hospitals, three state government hospitals, and three private hospitals. In determining total Medicaid payments for inpatient services to compare to costs, we included nonadjusted regular payments and UPL supplemental payments. That is, we used the actual regular payments and did not adjust for the severity of the patients' illnesses.

Figure 11. Medicaid Payments Compared with Medicaid Costs for Inpatient Hospital Services in One State, for Selected Hospitals with the Highest Daily Payments, State Fiscal Year 2011.

Medicaid: Key Issues Facing the Program 31

States are not required to limit Medicaid payments to a provider's costs of delivering Medicaid services, but Medicaid payments that greatly exceed a provider's Medicaid costs—and in some cases the providers' total operating costs—raise questions about whether those payments are economical and efficient, and are actually used for Medicaid purposes.

- Based on our analysis of the limited hospital-specific information that was available, we reported in 2012 that 39 states had made certain types of Medicaid supplemental payments to 505 hospitals that, along with their regular Medicaid payments, exceeded those hospitals' total costs of providing Medicaid-funded care by $2.7 billion.[47]

- Our recent analysis of CMS and state data we were able to obtain and analyze on provider payments to individual hospitals in two states found that average daily payment amounts—which reflect both regular payments and supplemental payments—varied widely among both government and private hospitals.[48] We again identified hospitals for which Medicaid payments received exceeded their Medicaid costs, and also found a few cases where states made payments to local government hospitals that exceeded the hospitals' total operating costs.[49] (See figure 11 for Medicaid payments compared with Medicaid costs in selected hospitals in one state.)

The lack of reliable provider-specific payment information is part of a broader challenge in assessing trends and patterns in program spending. Robust information on program spending, such as on aggregate spending trends and per-enrollee spending growth, is needed to ensure fiscal accountability, facilitate efforts to manage costs, and inform federal decision-making. CMS's two primary data sets that capture and report Medicaid expenditures—the CMS-64, which aggregates states' expenditures, and the Medicaid Statistical Information System (MSIS), which is designed to report individual beneficiary claims data—have the potential to offer a robust view of Medicaid spending.[50] However, their usefulness is limited because of issues with the completeness, accuracy, timeliness, and consistency of their data.[51] The MSIS data set, for example, does not contain complete information on supplemental payments. In addition, states have not consistently submitted timely MSIS information. Although CMS requires states to report data in MSIS within 45 days after a quarter has ended, states have often been late reporting MSIS data, and in some cases have delayed reporting for as long as 3 years. Also, total Medicaid expenditures—nationally and by state—often differ widely between the MSIS and CMS-64 data sets, even after accounting for differences between the data sets and the types of information provided.

CMS has taken a number of steps to improve the transparency and oversight of program payments and the data available to assess trends in program spending, as shown in the following examples.

- In 2008, CMS issued a final rule to implement additional reporting and audit requirements regarding DSH supplemental payments, which identified areas where states' payments were not consistent with federal requirements.[52]
- The agency is developing an enhanced Medicaid claims data system—called the Transformed Medicaid Statistical Information System (T-MSIS)—which agency officials expect will address many identified data issues and better facilitate oversight. CMS will require states to report information not currently collected in MSIS on certain Medicaid payments, such as provider-specific supplemental payments. States will also be required to report data more frequently.[53] It is uncertain when all states will be capable of reporting information via T-MSIS. As of December 2014, 18 states were in the final phases of testing, but it was uncertain when they would be ready for full implementation.[54]
- In 2014, CMS contracted for a study to, among other things, analyze documentation on supplemental payments to help identify opportunities to improve agency oversight.[55] In March 2015, CMS officials reported that the results of the analysis were not yet available.

Additional steps are needed to improve the transparency and oversight of program payments. In 2012, CMS said that expanding reporting and audit requirements for Medicaid UPL and other non-DSH supplemental payments would require legislation, and we have suggested that Congress consider requiring CMS to take similar steps to improve the transparency and accountability of these payments, including requiring annual reporting and independent auditing of supplemental payments states make to individual facilities.[56] While CMS's T-MSIS initiative could yield additional information on provider payments, data limitations and challenges will continue to limit CMS's ability to oversee these payments unless they are addressed.[57] We recommended that CMS improve its oversight by taking steps to ensure that

Medicaid: Key Issues Facing the Program 33

states report accurate provider- specific payment data, and by developing a policy and process for reviewing payments to individual providers to determine whether they are economical and efficient, and HHS concurred with our recommendations.[58]

Data on State Financing Sources

The Medicaid program involves significant and growing expenditures for the federal government and the states, and states have used various sources of funds to help finance the nonfederal share of the program.[59] These sources include funds from hospitals and other providers who serve Medicaid enrollees, such as through provider taxes, and funds from local governments and the health care entities they operate, such as local government hospitals or county nursing homes. States have considerable flexibility in determining which sources of funds to use to finance their nonfederal share. However, federal law does impose certain limits on the financing of overall Medicaid expenditures and sets parameters for certain funding sources, such as provider taxes. For example, under federal law, states must use state funds to finance at least 40 percent of the nonfederal share of total Medicaid expenditures each year.[60] In addition, when levying a provider tax, states must not hold providers harmless (e.g., must not provide a direct or indirect guarantee that providers will receive their money back).[61]

Trends toward increasing reliance on Medicaid providers and other non-state sources to fund the nonfederal share of Medicaid payments can effectively shift costs to the federal government. In 2014, we found that states are increasingly relying on providers and local governments to help fund Medicaid. For example, in state fiscal year 2012, funds from providers and local governments accounted for 26 percent (or over $46 billion) of the approximately $180 billion in the total nonfederal share of Medicaid payments that year—an increase from 21 percent ($31 billion) in state fiscal year 2008.[62] (See figure 12.)

Our work illustrates how this increased reliance on non-state sources of funds can shift costs from states to the federal government, changing the nature of the federal-state partnership. For example, we reported in 2014 that in one state a $220 million payment increase for nursing facilities (which was funded by a tax on nursing facilities) resulted in an estimated $110 million increase in federal matching funds; no increase in state general funds; and a net payment increase to the facilities, after paying the taxes, of $105 million.[63] (See figure 13.)

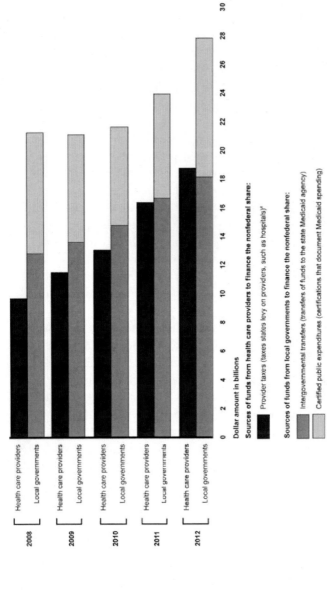

Source: GAO |GAO-15-677

[a] For this graphic, we use the term provider tax to refer to health care provider taxes, fees, or assessments. The amounts of provider taxes reported include provider donations. Provider donations totaled $17 million in 2008, $16 million in 2009, $78 million in 2010, $69 million in 2011, and $72 million in 2012.

Figure 12. Amount of the Nonfederal Share of Medicaid Payments from Health Care Providers and Local Governments, State Fiscal Years 2008 through 2012.

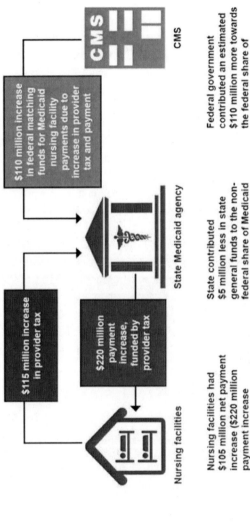

Source: GAO│GAO-15-677

Note: This figure illustrates the estimated effect of a new provider tax and increased Medicaid payments to nursing facilities, and on net Medicaid payments to nursing facilities in one state in state fiscal year 2012. For the analysis, we compared actual payments in that year to what payments would have been without the provider tax and increased Medicaid payments to nursing facilities.

[a] The state used state general funds to finance most of the nonfederal share of Medicaid, but we estimated that the provider tax resulted in the state needing to use $5 million less in state general funds to finance its share of Medicaid.

Figure 13. Example of How One State's Use of Non-State Sources to Fund Medicaid Payments to Nursing Facilities Shifted Medicaid Costs to the Federal Government in State Fiscal Year 2012.

Due to data limitations, CMS is not well-positioned to either identify states' Medicaid financing sources or assess their impact. Apart from data on provider taxes, CMS generally does not require (or otherwise collect) information from states on the funds they use to finance Medicaid, nor ensure that the data that it does collect are accurate and complete. The lack of transparency in states' sources of funds and financing arrangements hinders CMS's and federal policymakers' efforts to oversee Medicaid. Further, it is difficult to determine whether a state's increased reliance on funds from providers and local governments primarily serves to (1) provide fiscal relief to the state by increasing federal funding, or (2) increase payments to providers that in turn help improve beneficiary access.

CMS has recognized the need for better data from states on how they finance their share of Medicaid, and taken steps to collect some data, but additional steps are needed. We recommended in July 2014 that CMS take steps to ensure that states report accurate and complete information on all sources of funds used to finance the nonfederal share of Medicaid, and offered suggestions for doing so. HHS did not concur with our recommendation or suggestions, stating that its current efforts were adequate; however, HHS acknowledged that additional data were needed to ensure that states comply with federal requirements regarding how much local governments may contribute to the nonfederal share, and stated that it would examine efforts to improve data collection for oversight.[64] Given states' increased reliance on non-state sources to fund the nonfederal share of Medicaid, which can result in costs shifting to the federal government, we continue to believe that improved data are needed to improve transparency and oversight, such as to understand how increased federal costs may affect beneficiaries and the providers who serve them.

Improving HHS's Review and Approval Process for Demonstration Spending May Prevent Unnecessary Federal Spending

Another important element of ensuring Medicaid's fiscal accountability is improving HHS's policy, process, and criteria for approving state spending on demonstrations to ensure that (1) demonstrations will not significantly increase federal spending for Medicaid, and (2) demonstration spending furthers Medicaid objectives. The Secretary of HHS has broad authority under section 1115 of the Social Security Act to waive certain federal Medicaid requirements and allow costs that would not otherwise be eligible for federal matching funds for experimental, pilot, or demonstration projects that, in the Secretary's judgment, are likely to assist in promoting Medicaid objectives.[65]

Medicaid: Key Issues Facing the Program

These demonstrations account for a significant and growing proportion of federal Medicaid expenditures, accounting for close to one-third of total Medicaid expenditures in fiscal year 2014.[66]

Improvements to Transparency and Oversight to Ensure Budget Neutrality

Over the years, we have highlighted the need for improvement in HHS's criteria, policy, and process for approving states' demonstration spending limits. HHS policy requires that section 1115 demonstrations be budget-neutral to the federal government—that is, that demonstrations should not increase federal spending over what it would have been if the state's existing Medicaid program had continued.[67] However, HHS has approved demonstration spending limits that we estimate were billions of dollars higher than what federal spending would have been if the states' existing Medicaid programs had continued.[68] We found that HHS has allowed states to use questionable methods and assumptions for their spending baselines and growth rates without providing adequate documentation to support them.

- In 2013, we reported that HHS's approval documentation for 4 of 10 demonstrations we reviewed lacked evidence to justify proposed spending limits that were based on spending baselines and growth rates that greatly deviated from HHS's benchmarks.[69] For example, HHS approved a state's spending limit that included hypothetical costs rather than actual expenditures in the spending baseline.[70] If HHS had held spending limits in the 4 demonstrations to levels suggested by its budget neutrality policy, we estimated that the spending limits would have been $32 billion—$21 billion in federal funds—lower over the 5-year term of the demonstrations.

- Our 2014 review of HHS's process for approving Arkansas's Medicaid expansion demonstration spending limit found that HHS approved a spending limit for the demonstration that was based, in part, on hypothetical costs.[71] The hypothetical costs assumed that the state would make significantly higher payment amounts to providers if it expanded coverage under its traditional Medicaid program—and HHS did not request any data to support the state's assumptions. We estimated that the 3-year, nearly $4 billion spending limit that HHS approved for the Arkansas demonstration was approximately $778 million more than what the spending limit would have been if it were based on the state's actual payment rates for services provided to adult enrollees under the traditional Medicaid program.

Arkansas was the first state HHS approved to test whether providing premium assistance to purchase private coverage offered on the health insurance exchange would improve access for newly eligible Medicaid enrollees. HHS also authorized Arkansas and 11 other states to seek additional federal dollars beyond their approved spending limits should their actual costs prove higher than expected. This set another precedent, further eroding the integrity of HHS's process and increasing the risk of increased costs to the federal government.[72]

We have also found that HHS's policy was inconsistent with its actual practices and was not adequately documented. For example, while HHS policy requires that states submit 5 years of historical data in developing spending limits, the agency's current processes allowed states to use data based on the state's estimate of spending or enrollment. Officials indicated that if estimates are used instead of actual data, the state must explain any adjustments. But HHS officials did not have documentation for the current process or policy on when estimates are allowed, or the type of documentation of adjustments that is required.[73]

In recent years, both Congress and HHS have taken significant steps to improve the demonstration review and approval process by establishing a public input process at the federal level before demonstrations are approved,[74] and we believe more can be done. We have made a number of recommendations to HHS to improve the budget neutrality process by improving its review criteria and methods, and by documenting and making clear the basis for approved spending limits. In 2008, because HHS disagreed that our recommended changes were needed— maintaining that its review and approval process were sufficient—we suggested that Congress consider requiring the Secretary of HHS to improve the process by, for example, better ensuring that valid methods are used to demonstrate budget neutrality, and documenting and making public the basis for such approvals. In 2013, we further recommended that HHS update its written budget neutrality policy to reflect the actual criteria and processes used to develop and approve demonstration spending limits, and ensure the policy is readily available to state Medicaid directors and others. HHS acknowledged that it had not always communicated its budget neutrality policy broadly or clearly, but stated it had applied its policy consistently. HHS disagreed with our recommendation and noted that it had taken steps to improve transparency, such as by releasing in

2012 a demonstration application template that provided guidance on some of the data elements commonly used to demonstrate budget neutrality. We reported, however, that the application template was optional for states, did not address how HHS reviews the applications or the criteria used to set spending limits, and fell short of clarifying HHS's budget neutrality policy. HHS also disagreed with our 2013 and 2014 findings that it had approved demonstrations that may not be budget neutral, maintaining that its approvals were consistent with its policy and based on the best available data. However, given our findings and the variation and levels of federal spending in demonstrations that we reviewed, we continue to believe that HHS must take actions to improve the transparency and accountability of its demonstration approvals and should fully implement our recommendations.

Improvements to Criteria for and Documentation of How Demonstration Spending Furthers Medicaid Objectives

Our 2015 review of HHS's demonstration approvals found that HHS has not issued explicit criteria explaining how it determines that demonstration spending furthers Medicaid objectives, and that HHS's approval documents are not always clear as to what, precisely, approved expenditures are for and how they will promote these objectives.[75] Based on our review of all 25 states' approval documents for new, extended, or amended section 1115 demonstrations approved by HHS between June 2012 and October 2013, we found that HHS approved expenditure authorities for a broad range of purposes beyond Medicaid coverage, some of which appeared only tangentially related to improving health coverage for low-income individuals. For example, in five states, HHS approved expenditure authorities allowing the states to claim $9.5 billion in federal Medicaid funding for costs under about 150 state programs that would not otherwise have been eligible for federal Medicaid funding.[76] These programs were operated or funded by a wide range of state agencies, such as state departments of mental health, aging, or developmental disabilities that may also be receiving non-Medicaid federal grants and funds. Taken together, these actions committed the federal government to tens of billions in spending for costs not otherwise eligible for Medicaid.

Without clear criteria for assessing how states' proposed expenditure authorities will promote Medicaid objectives, and without clear documentation of the application of those criteria, the bases for HHS's decisions involving tens of billions of Medicaid dollars are not transparent to Congress, the states, or the public. We recommended that HHS issue criteria for assessing whether section 1115 expenditure authorities are likely to promote Medicaid objectives. HHS partially concurred with the recommendation on issuing criteria, saying that all section 1115 demonstrations are reviewed against "general criteria" to determine whether Medicaid objectives are met, including whether the demonstration will increase and strengthen coverage of low-income individuals. However, HHS has not issued these general criteria in writing, and we maintain that written and more-specific guidance is needed to improve transparency. In addition, we recommended that HHS ensure that the use of these criteria is documented in its approvals of demonstrations, and also take steps to ensure that its approval documentation consistently provide assurances that states will avoid duplicative spending (duplication between federal Medicaid funds for demonstrations and other federal funds available to states for the same or similar purposes). HHS concurred with both of these recommendations and committed to taking additional steps to require that demonstration approval documents more clearly articulate how section 1115 authority is being used to help states address evolving trends or needs in their Medicaid programs, as well as provide assurances that states will avoid duplication of federal spending.[77]

Improving Program Integrity

The federal government and the states both play important roles in ensuring that Medicaid payments made to health care providers and managed care organizations are correct and appropriate. The size and diversity of the Medicaid program make it particularly vulnerable to improper payments—including payments made for treatments or services that were not covered by program rules, that were not medically necessary, or that were billed for but never provided. Medicaid improper payments are a significant cost to Medicaid—totaling an estimated $17.5 billion in fiscal year 2014, according to HHS. Due to our concerns about Medicaid's improper payment rate and the sufficiency of federal and state oversight, we added Medicaid to our list of high-risk programs in 2003.[78] An effective federal-state partnership is key to ensuring the most appropriate use of funds by (1) identifying and preventing improper payments in both fee-for-service and managed care, (2) setting appropriate payment rates for managed care organizations, and (3) ensuring only eligible individuals and providers participate in Medicaid.

- Additional actions needed to identify and prevent improper payments.
- Ongoing efforts to improve oversight of managed care payment rates are important for ensuring rates are appropriate.
- Efforts to ensure only eligible individuals and providers participate in Medicaid can be improved.

Source: GAO. | GAO-15-677

Additional Actions Needed to Identify and Prevent Improper Payments

Responsibility for program integrity activities is spread across multiple state and federal entities, resulting in fragmented efforts, creating the potential for unnecessary duplication, which we have previously identified in some areas, as well as program areas not being covered. The combined federal and state efforts have recovered only a small portion of the estimated improper payments in Medicaid, and the Medicaid improper payment rate has recently increased.[79] These factors, coupled with recent and projected increases in Medicaid spending, heighten the importance of coordinated and cost-effective program integrity efforts. CMS has taken many important steps in recent years to help improve program integrity— including some in response to our recommendations—and we believe even more can be done in this area.

Coordinating to Minimize Duplication and Ensure Coverage

Our work has highlighted how careful coordination of federal and state efforts is necessary to both avoid duplication and ensure maximum program coverage. Given the number of entities involved in program integrity efforts, coordination among entities is critical. (See figure 14.) Without careful coordination, the involvement of multiple state and federal entities in Medicaid program integrity results in fragmented efforts, possibly leaving some program areas insufficiently covered.

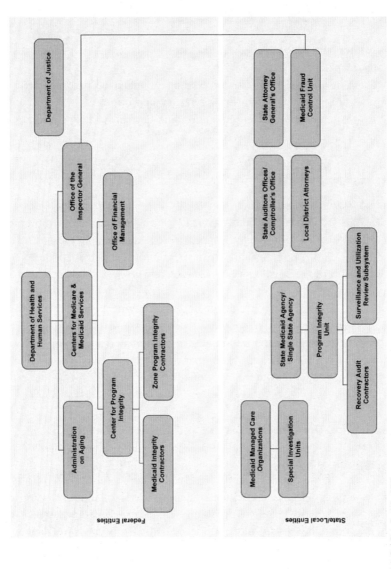

Source: GAO |GAO-15-677

Figure 14. Federal and Non-Federal Entities with Primary Oversight Responsibilities for Medicaid Program Integrity.

Medicaid: Key Issues Facing the Program 43

In 2014, we reported a gap in oversight of the growing expenditures on Medicaid managed care, which constituted over a quarter of federal Medicaid expenditures in 2011. In particular, we found that the federal government and the states were not well positioned to identify improper payments made to—or by—managed care organizations.[80] We found that CMS had largely delegated managed care program integrity oversight activities to the states, but states generally focused their efforts on fee-for-service claims. We concluded that further federal and state oversight, coupled with additional federal guidance and support to states, could help ensure that managed care organizations are taking appropriate actions to identify and prevent improper payments. Specifically, we recommended that CMS

1. require states to conduct audits of payments to and by managed care organizations;
2. update CMS's Medicaid managed care guidance on program integrity practices and effective handling of recoveries by managed care plans; and
3. provide states with additional support in overseeing Medicaid managed care program integrity, such as the option to obtain audit assistance from existing Medicaid integrity contractors.

CMS generally agreed with our recommendations, and has taken steps to provide states with additional guidance. In October 2014, CMS made available on its website the managed care plan compliance toolkit to provide further guidance to states and managed care plans on identifying improper payments to providers. In addition, agency officials told us that, as of December 2014, at least six states were using their audit contractors to audit managed care claims. While CMS has taken steps to improve oversight of Medicaid managed care, the lack of a comprehensive program integrity strategy for managed care leaves a growing portion of Medicaid funds at risk. In our view, CMS actions to require states to conduct audits of payments to and by managed care organizations, and to update guidance on Medicaid managed care program integrity practices and recoveries, are crucial to improving program integrity, and we will continue to follow CMS's actions in this area. (Appendix I includes our open recommendations regarding Medicaid improper payments, which we believe could help reduce improper payments if implemented.)

On June 1, 2015, the agency issued a proposed rule to revise program integrity policies, including policy measures that we have recommended.[81] Among other measures, if finalized, the rule would require states to conduct audits of managed care organizations' encounter and financial data every three years. Additionally, the proposed rule would standardize the treatment of recovered overpayments by plans.

Identifying Cost-Effective Efforts

Our work has highlighted the importance of focusing state and federal resources on cost-effective efforts to identify improper payments. States' information systems are a key component of program integrity activities, and states' program integrity efforts include

- enrolling providers;
- receiving, reviewing, and paying Medicaid claims; and
- auditing claims payments after the fact.

Consistent with the requirements defined by CMS, states use Medicaid Management Information Systems (MMIS) provider and claims processing subsystems to perform program integrity activities related to provider enrollment and prepayment review. (See figure 15.)

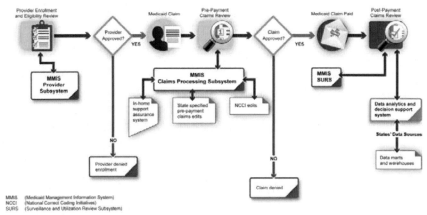

Source: GAO analysis based on Centers for Medicare & Medicaid Services and states' data. | GAO-15-677

Figure 15. Overview of Selected States' Program Integrity Activities and Supporting MMIS and Additional Systems.

Our work has shown that the effectiveness of states' information systems used for program integrity purposes is uncertain.[82] In 2015, we reviewed 10 states' use of information technology systems to support efforts aimed at preventing and detecting improper payments. These states' information systems ranged in age and capability, with 3 of the 10 states' operating systems being more than 20 years old. However, the effectiveness of the states' use of the systems for program integrity purposes is not known, and we recommended that CMS require states to measure and report quantifiable benefits of program integrity systems when requesting federal funds, and to reflect their approach for doing so. CMS concurred with these recommendations.

In our past work, we also recommended—and CMS acted on—other measures to streamline program integrity efforts, as shown in the following examples.[83]

- CMS's hiring of separate review and audit contractors for its program integrity efforts was inefficient and led to duplication because key functions—such as assessing whether payments were improper and learning states' Medicaid policies—were performed by both contractors. We recommended that CMS eliminate duplication between the separate contractors, which CMS did in conjunction with the agency's redesign of its Medicaid Integrity Program. This redesign eliminated the review contractor function and included a more collaborative and coordinated audit approach that leverages state expertise to identify potential audit targets, and relies on more complete and up-to-date state Medicaid claims data.
- Two CMS oversight tools—the state comprehensive reviews and the state program integrity assessments—were duplicative because both tools were used to collect similar information from the states. Furthermore, we found that the state program integrity assessments contained unverified and inaccurate data. We recommended that CMS eliminate this duplication, and CMS subsequently discontinued the state program integrity assessments.
- CMS's comprehensive reviews of states' program integrity efforts contained important information about all aspects of states' program integrity capabilities.[84] However, we found no apparent connection between the reviews' findings and CMS's selection of states for audits. We recommended that CMS use the knowledge gained from the comprehensive reviews as a criterion for focusing audit resources

toward states with structural or data-analysis vulnerabilities. CMS agreed and, among other steps, in 2013 redesigned the reviews to streamline the process, reduce the burden on states, and refocus the reviews on risk-assessment.

Ensuring Medicaid Remains a Payer of Last Resort

CMS and the states must ensure that if Medicaid enrollees have another source of health care coverage, that source should pay, to the extent of its liability, before Medicaid does. Medicaid enrollees may have health care coverage through third parties—such as private health insurers—for a number of reasons. For example, some adults may be covered by employer-sponsored insurance even though they qualify for Medicaid. Similarly, children may be eligible for Medicaid while being covered under a parent's health plan. Figure 16 shows the estimated prevalence of private health insurance among Medicaid enrollees.

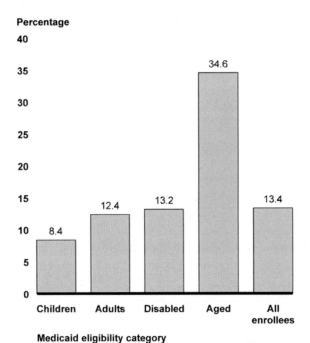

Source: GAO analysis of 2012 U.S. Census Bureau data. | GAO-15-677

Figure 16. Estimated Prevalence of Private Health Insurance among Medicaid Enrollees by Eligibility Category, 2012.

In 2015, we found that states had adopted various approaches to identify enrollees with other insurance than Medicaid, and states were working to ensure that these third parties paid for health care services to the extent of their liability before Medicaid. However, these states needed additional CMS guidance and support in these efforts.[85] We recommended that CMS play a more active leadership role in monitoring, supporting, and promoting state third-party liability efforts. Specifically, we recommended that CMS

1. routinely monitor and share across all states information regarding key third-party liability efforts and challenges, and
2. provide guidance to states on their oversight of third-party liability efforts conducted by Medicaid managed care plans.

CMS concurred with our recommendations, and stated that it would continue to look at ways to provide guidance to states to allow for sharing of effective practices and to increase awareness of initiatives under development in states. CMS also stated that it would explore the need for additional guidance regarding state oversight of third-party liability efforts conducted by Medicaid managed care plans. In the preamble to the June 1, 2015, proposed rule, the agency indicated it plans to issue guidance, which would require managed care plans to include information on third-party liability amounts in the encounter data submitted to states. We will continue to follow CMS's actions in this area.

Ongoing Efforts to Improve Oversight of Managed Care Payment Rates Are Important for Ensuring Rates Are Appropriate

Managed care is designed to ensure the provision of appropriate health care services in a cost-efficient manner. However, the design of capitation payments, which are made prospectively to health plans to provide or arrange for services for Medicaid enrollees, can create incentives that adversely affect program integrity and patient care. For example, these payments may create an incentive to underserve or deny access to needed care. Thus, appropriate safeguards are needed to ensure access to care and appropriate payment in Medicaid managed care.[86]

In 2010, we found that CMS's oversight of states' Medicaid managed care rate setting methodologies was not consistent across its regional offices, and that in assessing the quality of the data used to set rates, the agency primarily relied on state and health plan assurances, thereby placing billions of federal and state dollars at risk.[87] We found significant gaps in CMS's oversight. For example, in one instance, the agency had not reviewed one state's rate setting for multiple years, resulting in the state receiving approximately $5 billion a year in federal funds for three years without having had its rates reviewed by CMS. We also found that regional offices varied in their interpretations of how extensive a review of states' rate setting was needed and the sufficiency of evidence for meeting actuarial soundness requirements, among other things. We recommended that CMS

1. implement a mechanism to track state compliance with requirements,
2. clarify guidance on rate-setting reviews, and
3. make use of information on data quality in determining the appropriateness of managed care capitation rates.

As a result of our work, CMS implemented a detailed checklist to standardize the regional offices' reviews. CMS has also taken a number of other steps to improve its oversight of states' rate setting.

- In 2014, CMS completed its development of a database to track contracts, including rate-setting reviews. According to agency officials, as of March 2015, 57 rate submissions had been submitted to the database and were undergoing review by CMS's Office of the Actuary and the Division of Managed Care Plans.
- CMS officials reported that the agency had developed a managed care program review manual, which included modules on financial oversight, and had updated rate setting and contract review tools.
- In 2014, the agency released its 2015 Managed Care Rate Setting Consultation Guide, which clarified the agency's requirements relating to the information states must submit in developing their rate certifications, including a description of the type, sources, and quality of the data used by the state in setting its rates.
- On June 1, 2015, the agency issued a proposed rule that, if finalized, would make changes to Medicaid managed care rate setting, such as requiring more consistent and transparent documentation of the rate setting process to allow for more effective reviews of states' rate certification submissions. We will continue to follow CMS's actions in this area.

Efforts to Ensure Only Eligible Individuals and Providers Participate in Medicaid Can Be Improved

Both CMS and the states play an important role in ensuring that only eligible individuals receive Medicaid coverage and that only eligible providers receive payment. Our work has highlighted several issues facing CMS and the states in their efforts to minimize fraud in Medicaid eligibility among both enrollees and providers.

To be eligible for Medicaid coverage, applicants must meet financial and nonfinancial requirements, such as federal and state requirements regarding residency, immigration status, and documentation of U.S. citizenship. Similarly, to participate in Medicaid, providers must enroll and submit information about their ownership interests and criminal background. States must screen potential Medicaid providers, search exclusion and debarment lists, and take action to exclude those providers who appear on those lists.[88] Using 2011 data, we recently identified indications of potentially fraudulent or improper payments related to certain Medicaid enrollees and paid to some providers, as shown in our review of approximately 9 million enrollees in four states and summarized below.[89] While these cases indicate only potentially improper payments, they raise questions about the effectiveness of beneficiary and provider enrollment screening controls.[90]

- We identified about 8,600 enrollees who had payments made on their behalf concurrently by two or more of our selected states.[91] Medicaid approved benefits of at least $18.3 million for these enrollees in these states.
- We identified about 200 deceased enrollees in the four states who appear to have received Medicaid benefits totaling at least $9.6 million. Specifically, our analysis matching Medicaid data to the Social Security Administration's data on date of death found these individuals were deceased before the Medicaid service was provided.
- We found that about 50 medical providers in the four states we examined had been excluded from federal health care programs, including Medicaid; these providers were excluded from these programs when they provided and billed for Medicaid services during fiscal year 2011. The selected states approved the claims at a cost of about $60,000.
- We found that the identities of over 50 deceased providers in the four states we examined were used to receive Medicaid payments. Our analysis matching Medicaid eligibility and claims data to the Social

50 United States Government Accountability Office

Security Administration's full death file found these individuals were deceased before the Medicaid service was provided. The Medicaid benefits involved with these deceased providers totaled at least $240,000 for fiscal year 2011.

- We found nearly 26,600 providers with addresses that did not match any U.S. Postal Service records. These unknown addresses may have errors due to inaccurate data entry or differences in the ages of MMIS and U.S. Postal Service address-management tool data, making it difficult to determine whether these cases involve fraud through data matching alone.

CMS has taken steps since 2011 to strengthen the Medicaid beneficiary and provider enrollment-screening controls in ways that may address the issues we identified, and we believe that additional CMS guidance could bolster those efforts.[92] In 2013, CMS issued federal regulations, in response to PPACA, to establish a more rigorous approach to verify the information needed to determine Medicaid eligibility. Under these regulations, states are required to use electronic data maintained by the federal government to the extent that such information may be useful in verifying eligibility. CMS created a tool called the Data Services Hub, implemented in fiscal year 2014, to help verify some of the information used to determine eligibility for Medicaid and other health programs. States are to use the hub to both verify an individual's eligibility when they receive an application, and to reverify eligibility on at least an annual basis thereafter, unless the state has an alternative mechanism approved by HHS.[93] In addition, in February 2011, CMS and HHS's Office of Inspector General issued regulations establishing a new risk-based screening process for providers with enhanced verification measures, such as unscheduled or unannounced site visits and fingerprint-based criminal background checks. If properly implemented by CMS, the hub and the additional provider screening measures could help mitigate some of the potential improper payment issues that we identified. However, we identified gaps in state practices for identifying deceased enrollees, as well as state challenges in screening providers effectively and efficiently,[94] and recommended that CMS provide guidance to states to better

1. identify enrollees who are deceased, and
2. screen providers by using automated information available through Medicare's enrollment database.

HHS concurred with our recommendations and stated it would work with states to determine additional approaches to better identify deceased enrollees, and that it would continue to educate states about the availability of provider information and how to use that information to help screen Medicaid providers more effectively and efficiently. We will continue to monitor HHS's efforts in this area.

Addressing Variations in States' Financing Needs through Revised Federal Financing Approach

Medicaid's federal-state partnership could be improved through a revised federal financing approach that better addresses variations in states' financing needs. First, automatically providing increased federal financial assistance to states affected by national economic downturns—through an increased FMAP—could help provide timely and targeted assistance that is more responsive to states' economic conditions. Second, revisions to the current FMAP formula could more equitably allocate Medicaid funds to states by better accounting for their ability to fund Medicaid. These improvements could better align federal funding with each state's resources, demand for services, and costs; better facilitate state budget planning; and provide states with greater fiscal stability during times of economic stress.

- More timely and targeted federal assistance would better aid states during economic downturns.
- More equitable funding formula would better reflect states' varying ability to fund Medicaid.

Source: GAO. | GAO-15-677

More Timely and Targeted Federal Assistance Would Better Aid States during Economic Downturns

Economic downturns can hamper states' ability to fund their Medicaid programs. During economic downturns, states' employment and tax revenues typically fall, while enrollment in the Medicaid program tends to increase as the number of individuals with incomes low enough to qualify for Medicaid coverage rises. We have reported that each state, however, can experience different economic circumstances—and thus different levels of change in Medicaid enrollment and state revenues during a downturn.[95] Figures 17 and 18 show the percentage change in Medicaid enrollment and state tax revenue, by state, respectively.

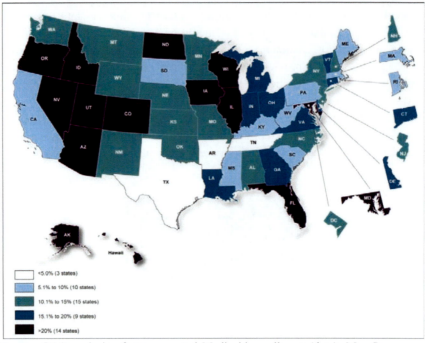

Source: GAO analysis of state reported Medicaid enrollment (data); Map Resources (map). | GAO-15-677

Notes: Percentages are based on GAO analysis of Medicaid enrollment data from December 2007 through December 2009 as reported by state Medicaid directors.
For the purpose of this figure, "states" includes the District of Columbia.

Figure 17. Percentage Change in Medicaid Enrollment, December 2007 through December 2009.

Medicaid: Key Issues Facing the Program 53

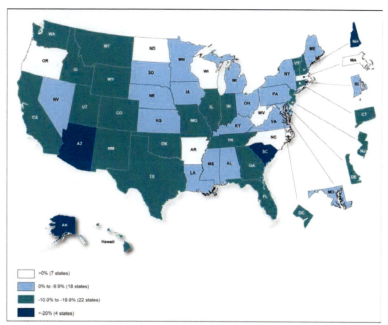

Source: GAO analysis of U.S. Census revenue (data); Map Resources (map). | GAO-15-677

Notes: Map shows the total percent change in quarterly tax revenue for each state from the fourth quarter 2007 to the fourth quarter 2009.

For the purpose of this figure, "states" includes the District of Columbia.

Figure 18. Percentage Change in State Tax Revenue, Fourth Quarter 2007 to Fourth Quarter 2009.

In response to the two most recent recessions, Congress acted to temporarily increase support to states by increasing the federal share of Medicaid funding provided by the FMAP formula.

- Following the 2001 recession, the Jobs and Growth Tax Relief Reconciliation Act of 2003 provided states $10 billion in temporary assistance through an increased FMAP.[96]
- In response to the 2007 recession, the American Recovery and Reinvestment Act of 2009 (Recovery Act) provided states with $89 billion through a temporarily increased FMAP. Under the Recovery Act, the level of funding was intended to help both maintain state Medicaid programs so enrollees would be assured continuity of services—and to assist states with fiscal needs beyond Medicaid.[97]

Our prior work, however, found that these efforts to provide states with temporary increases in the FMAP were not as responsive to states' economic conditions as they could have been.[98] Improving the responsiveness of federal assistance to states during economic downturns would facilitate state budget planning, provide states with greater fiscal stability, and better align federal assistance with the magnitude of the economic downturn's effects on individual states. We have identified opportunities to improve the timing, amount, and duration of assistance provided,[99] as detailed below.

- **Automatic and timely trigger for starting assistance**. To be effective at stabilizing state funding of Medicaid programs, assistance should be provided close to the beginning of a downturn. An automatically activated, prearranged mechanism for triggering federal assistance could use readily available economic data to begin assistance rather than rely on legislative action at the time of a future national economic downturn.
- **Targeted assistance based on state needs**. States' efforts to fund Medicaid during economic downturns face two main challenges: (1) financing increased enrollment, and (2) replacing lost revenue. We found that better targeting of assistance based on each state's level of need could help ensure that federal assistance is aligned with the magnitude of an economic downturn's effect on individual states.
- **Timely and tapered end of assistance**. Determining when and how to end increased FMAP assistance to states is complicated.[100] We found that more gradually reducing the percentage of increased FMAP provided to states could help mitigate the effects of a slower recovery. Such tapered assistance would avoid abrupt changes and allow states to plan their transitions back to greater reliance on their own revenues.

The Recovery Act included a provision for GAO to provide recommendations for modifying the increased FMAP formula to make it more responsive to state Medicaid needs during future economic downturns. In response to the provision, we presented a prototype formula that offers an option for temporary FMAP increases that would provide automatic, timely, and targeted state assistance.[101] Our prototype formula would use labor market data—specifically, the employment-to- population (EPOP) ratio—as an automatic trigger to start and end the increased FMAP assistance.[102] Table 1 highlights design elements of our prototype formula, as well as related considerations for policymakers. The level of funding and other design elements—such as the choice of thresholds for starting, ending, and targeting assistance—are variables that policymakers could adjust depending on circumstances, such as competing budget demands and other state fiscal needs beyond Medicaid.

We compared this prototype formula with assistance provided during the Recovery Act. Under our prototype formula, assistance would have begun in January 2008 rather than in October 2008, as was the case under the Recovery Act; the end of assistance would have been triggered in April 2011, and assistance would have been phased out by September 2011, rather than in June 2011 under the Recovery Act and its extension.

Based on our work, we noted that Congress could consider enacting an FMAP formula that is targeted for variable state Medicaid needs and provides automatic, timely, and temporary increased FMAP assistance in response to national economic downturns. As of July 2015, Congress has not enacted such a formula. In commenting on drafts of our 2011 reports, HHS agreed with the analysis and goals of the reports, emphasized the importance of aligning changes to the FMAP formula with individual state circumstances, and offered several considerations to guide policy choices regarding appropriate thresholds for timing and targeting of increased FMAP funds.

More Equitable Funding Formula Would Better Reflect States' Varying Ability to Fund Medicaid

In prior work spanning more than three decades, we have emphasized that in federal-state programs such as Medicaid, funds should be allocated to states in a manner that is equitable from the perspective of both enrollees and taxpayers.[103]

- To be equitable from the perspective of enrollees, and thereby allow states to provide a comparable level of services to each person in need, a funding allocation mechanism should take into account the demand for services in each state—which depends on both the number of people needing services and their level of need—and geographic cost differences among states.
- To be equitable from the perspective of taxpayers, an allocation mechanism should ensure that taxpayers in poorer states are not more heavily burdened than those in wealthier ones. To account for states' relative wealth, a mechanism must take into account each state's ability to finance its share of program costs from its own resources,

which should account for all potentially taxable income, including personal income of state residents and corporate income.

Table 1. Key Design Choices Contained in GAO Prototype Formula and Policy Considerations

Design element	GAO prototype formula	Policy considerations
Starting assistance	Assistance automatically begins when 26 states have declining employment-to-population (EPOP) ratios over two consecutive months.	Choices need to balance offering prompt assistance against triggering assistance when there is greater assurance that a national recession has begun. Adjustments could be made to the • threshold number of states, and • number of months with a declining EPOP ratio.
Targeting assistance	Targeting is based on a state's minimum unemployment rate and maximum wage and salary quarter, as identified over the past eight quarters.	The look-back period for calculating changes in unemployment, and changes in wages and salaries could be changed, with trade-offs between overall program cost and timeliness of assistance.
Determining level of state need	Full funding for state Medicaid needs related to increased enrollment and decreased revenues.	Proportional scaling of the assistance could be implemented, scaling up to address broader state budget needs, or down to reduce program costs.
Ending assistance	Temporary assistance ends when fewer than 26 states show declining EPOPs over two consecutive months.	Choices need to balance premature shut-down of the assistance period against the costs of the assistance. Adjustments could be made to the threshold number of states and number of months with a declining EPOP.
Using a phased reduction to end assistance	Assistance ends with a phased reduction of FMAP increases, using a floating look-back period of eight quarters. After the first eight quarters of assistance, the look-back period is constrained to not exceed eight quarters.	To ensure that no state experiences a sharp decline in their temporary increased FMAP at the end of the period, a phase-out rule could constrain the quarterly drop in FMAP.

Source: GAO. | GAO-15-677

Our prior work has found that the current FMAP formula does not adequately address variation in the demand for services in each state, geographic cost differences, and state resources.[104] The FMAP formula uses per capita income as the basis for calculating each state's federal matching rate. However, per capita income is a poor proxy for the size of a state's population in need of Medicaid services, as two states with similar per capita incomes can have substantially different numbers of low-income residents.[105] Per capita income also does not include any measure of geographic differences in the costs of providing health care services, which can vary widely. Finally, although per capita income measures the income received by state residents—such as wages, rents, and interest income—it does not include other components of a state's resources that affect its ability to finance Medicaid, such as corporate income produced within the state, but not received by state residents.

In 2013, we identified multiple alternative data sources that could be used to develop measures of the demand for Medicaid services, geographic cost differences, and state resources.[106] These measures could be combined in various ways to provide a basis for allocating Medicaid funds more equitably among states. (See table 2.)

MEDICAID'S ONGOING TRANSFORMATION HIGHLIGHTS THE IMPORTANCE OF FEDERAL OVERSIGHT

We have reported over the years on challenges facing the Medicaid program and concerns about the adequacy of federal oversight. As previously discussed, in 2003, we designated Medicaid as a high-risk program due to its size, growth, diversity of programs, and concerns about gaps in oversight.[107] More than a decade later, those factors remain relevant for federal oversight. In addition, state Medicaid programs are changing rapidly. PPACA has led to unprecedented programmatic changes, and more are anticipated as states continue to pursue new options available under the law to expand eligibility and restructure payment and health care delivery systems. The effects of changes brought on by PPACA, as well as the aging of the U.S. population, will continue to emerge in the coming years and are likely to exacerbate the challenges that already exist in federal oversight and management of the Medicaid program.[108] In addition, other changes in states' health care delivery and payment approaches, as well as new technologies, will continue to pose challenges to federal oversight and management. These changes have implications for enrollees and for program costs, and underscore the importance of ongoing attention to federal oversight efforts.

Table 2. Alternative Data Sources that Could Improve Equity across States

Measure	Examples of possible data sources	How measures could improve equity across states
Demand for services	U.S. Census Bureau's American Community Survey and Current Population Survey	• Directly estimate the number of persons in each state with incomes low enough to qualify for Medicaid. • Estimates can be adjusted to reflect variation in health service needs within this population.
Geographic cost differences	Bureau of Labor Statistics' Occupational Employment Statistics Survey	• Account for components of health care costs and their variation across states. • Data source accounts for the cost of personnel who provide health care services (the greatest share of costs).
State resources	Department of Treasury's Total Taxable Resources	• Includes all types of income and is unaffected by an individual state's taxing authorities or policies. • In addition to per capita income, adds other sources of taxable income, such as income produced within a state, but received by individuals who reside out-of-state.

Source: GAO analysis. | GAO-15-677

Emerging changes brought on by PPACA will transform states' enrollment processes, as well as increase enrollment and program spending. Oversight to monitor access and use of services will be critical.

- **Enrollment processes**. PPACA required the establishment of a coordinated eligibility and enrollment process for Medicaid, CHIP, and the health insurance exchanges.[109] To implement this process— referred to as the "no wrong door" policy—states were required to develop IT systems that allow for the exchange of data to ensure that applicants are enrolled in the program for which they are eligible, regardless of the program for which they applied. We found that some states struggled with meeting the requirement to transfer—send and receive—applications with the federally facilitated exchange.[110]

- **Increased enrollment.** Enrollment is expected to increase significantly, even in states that do not implement the expansion, as streamlined processes and publicity about the expansion encourage enrollment among previously eligible but unenrolled adults and children. The sheer number of additional enrollees—about 10 million by 2020, according to Congressional Budget Office (CBO) estimates—may stretch health care resources and exacerbate challenges to ensuring access to care.[111]
- **Increased spending.** Over the next 5 years, Medicaid expenditures are expected to increase more rapidly than in the prior 10 years, rising from an estimated $529 billion in combined federal and state spending in 2015 to about $700 billion in 2020, due, in part, to the continuing implementation of PPACA.[112] The federal share of expenditures, which has historically averaged about 57 percent, is projected to increase as well, to about 60 percent, largely because of the enhanced federal match required under PPACA for newly eligible enrollees.

The expected increase in Medicaid enrollment and spending underscores the importance of addressing problems we have previously identified in ensuring fiscal accountability, program integrity, and access. For example, the large and growing number of Medicaid enrollees, coupled with previous challenges we have identified in monitoring and ensuring enrollees' access to care, underscore the importance of effective federal oversight efforts in this area. In addition, better data on Medicaid spending, including supplemental payments that states often make to institutional providers, would help to ensure the fiscal accountability and integrity of the program, facilitate efforts to manage program costs, and provide information needed for policy making.[113] Lastly, improved federal program integrity efforts will be critical to ensuring the appropriate use of program funds.

Continued increases in states' demonstration spending, changes in states' delivery systems and payment approaches, as well as the aging of the population and the introduction of new technologies also will continue to pose challenges to federal oversight.

- **Increased demonstration spending**. Medicaid spending governed by the terms and conditions of Medicaid demonstrations, rather than traditional Medicaid state plan requirements, accounted for close to one-third of federal Medicaid spending in 2014—up from one-fourth of federal Medicaid spending in 2013 and one-fifth in 2011.[114] The trend among states to seek flexibilities under the demonstration authority has implications for enrollees' access and program spending. For example, enrollees may lose protections—such as those to limit cost-sharing or to provide certain mandatory benefits—under the traditional Medicaid program. The federal government will need to oversee increasingly diverse Medicaid programs not subject to traditional Medicaid requirements. As of February 2015, HHS had approved demonstration proposals from two states—Arkansas and Iowa—allowing them to provide coverage to some or all of their expansion populations through premium assistance to purchase private health insurance on exchanges established under PPACA.[115]
- **Changes in states' delivery systems**. Growth of managed care and states' exploration of new models of health care delivery systems, particularly for long-term services and supports, will further heighten the need for program oversight.
  - Enrollment of Medicaid populations in managed care arrangements continues to grow, with attendant challenges for program oversight. Over the next 5 years, expenditures for capitation payments and premiums are projected to grow more rapidly than total Medicaid expenditures. We have found weaknesses in CMS and state oversight of managed care.[116] The HHS Office of Inspector General has also documented weaknesses in state standards, as well as significant issues with the availability of providers, and called for CMS to work with states to improve oversight of managed care plans.[117]
  - Recent state efforts to explore new health care models have implications for federal oversight of enrollees' care and program costs. In July 2012, CMS announced a major initiative to support state design and testing of innovative health care payment and service delivery models intended to enhance quality of care and lower costs for enrollees in Medicaid, CHIP, and Medicare, as well as other state residents. Beginning in 2017, states may

Medicaid: Key Issues Facing the Program

embark on even more ambitious efforts to reshape their payment and delivery systems.[118]

- The past two decades have seen a marked shift in where and how long term care services are delivered to disabled and aged enrollees, with care increasingly being provided in home- and community-based settings rather than in institutions such as nursing homes. In fiscal year 2011, about 45 percent of long term care spending was for home- and community-based services, up from 32 percent in 2002. As the population ages—and particularly as the number of people over age 85 increases—Medicaid expenditures on these services are predicted to grow.

- **New technology.** New developments in technology, such as innovations in health care treatments and telemedicine, are likely to influence how state Medicaid programs deliver and pay for care—raising implications for federal oversight of access to care and costs.
  - In 2008, CBO concluded from its review of the economic literature that roughly half of the increase in health care spending during the past several decades was associated with the expanded capabilities of medicine brought about by technological advances, including new drugs, devices, or services, as well as new clinical applications of existing technologies.[119]
  - The potential for new technologies to contribute significantly to long-term health care spending growth poses particular challenges for the Medicaid program. State Medicaid directors have highlighted as a critical concern the emergence of high-cost, cutting-edge pharmaceuticals, in light of the requirement that state Medicaid programs that cover outpatient drugs must cover nearly all Food and Drug Administration-approved prescription drugs of manufacturers that participate in the Medicaid drug rebate program.[120]

These changes underscore the importance of addressing problems we have identified in ensuring fiscal accountability, program integrity, and access. For example, as additional states submit demonstration proposals—and as the demonstrations HHS has already approved come up for renewal—the concerns and recommendations that we have raised about HHS approving demonstrations without assurances that they will not increase federal expenditures are likely to persist or increase.

The potential for sweeping changes in state Medicaid programs' payment and service delivery systems has implications for enrollees' access to and quality of care, and for program costs. Increasing enrollment in managed care arrangements may heighten concerns about access to care and program integrity within these arrangements. We have made recommendations to HHS that could help address concerns we have raised in these areas.

Attention to Medicaid's transformation and the key issues facing the program will be important to ensuring that Medicaid is both effective for the enrollees who rely on it and accountable to the taxpayers. GAO has multiple ongoing studies in these areas and will continue to monitor the Medicaid program for the Congress.

AGENCY COMMENTS

We provided a draft of this report to HHS for review. HHS provided technical comments, which we incorporated as appropriate.

Katherine M. Iritani
Director, Health Care

Carolyn L. Yocom
Director, Health Care

APPENDIX I: MEDICAID-RELATED MATTERS FOR CONGRESSIONAL CONSIDERATION AND AGENCY RECOMMENDATIONS

The following table lists Medicaid-related matters for congressional consideration GAO has published that are classified as open because Congress has either not taken or has not completed steps to implement the matter. The matters are listed by key issue and report.

Medicaid: Key Issues Facing the Program 63

Table 3. Open Medicaid-Related Matters for Congressional Consideration, by Key Issue, as of July 2015

GAO Report	Open Matters for Congressional Consideration
Ensuring Fiscal Accountability Through Increased Transparency and Oversight	
Medicaid: More Transparency of and Accountability for Supplemental Payments Are Needed. GAO-13-48, November 26, 2012	Congress should consider requiring the Centers for Medicare & Medicaid Services to 1. improve state reporting of non-disproportionate share hospital (DSH) supplemental payments, including requiring annual reporting of payments made to individual facilities and other information that the agency determines is necessary to oversee non-DSH supplemental payments; 2. clarify permissible methods for calculating non-DSH supplemental payments; and 3. require states to submit an annual independent certified audit verifying state compliance with permissible methods for calculating non-DSH supplemental payments.
Medicaid Demonstration Waivers: Recent HHS Approvals Continue to Raise Cost and Oversight Concerns. GAO-08-87, January 31, 2008	Congress may wish to consider requiring increased attention to fiscal responsibility in the approval of Section 1115 Medicaid demonstrations by requiring the Department of Health and Human Services (HHS) to improve the demonstration review process through steps such as clarifying criteria for reviewing and approving states' proposed spending limits; better ensuring that valid methods are used to demonstrate budget neutrality; and documenting and making public material explaining the basis for any approvals.
Addressing Variations in States' Financing Needs through Revised Federal Financing Approach	
Medicaid: Prototype Formula Would Provide Automatic, Targeted Assistance to States during Economic Downturns. GAO-12-38, November 10, 2011	Congress could consider enacting a Federal Medical Assistance Percentage (FMAP) formula that is targeted for variable state Medicaid needs and provides automatic, timely, and temporary increased FMAP assistance in response to national economic downturns.

Source: GAO. | GAO-15-677

The following table lists selected Medicaid-related recommendations GAO has made to the Department of Health and Human Services that are classified as open because the agency has either not taken or has not completed steps to implement the recommendation. The recommendations are listed by key issue and report.

Table 4. Selected Open Medicaid-Related Recommendations, by Key Issue, as of July 2015

GAO Report	Open Recommendation
Maintaining and Improving Access to Quality Care	
Foster Children: Additional Federal Guidance Could Help States Better Plan for Oversight of Psychotropic Medications Administered by Managed-Care Organizations. GAO-14-362, April 28, 2014	The Department of Health and Human Services (HHS) should issue guidance to state Medicaid, child-welfare, and mental-health officials regarding prescription-drug monitoring and oversight for children in foster care receiving psychotropic medications through managed care organizations (MCO).
Medicaid and CHIP: Reports for Monitoring Children's Health Care Services Need Improvement. GAO-11-293R, April 5, 2011	The Centers for Medicare & Medicaid Services (CMS) should work with states to identify additional improvements that could be made to the CMS 416 annual reports, including options for reporting on the receipt of services separately for children in managed care and fee-for-service delivery models, while minimizing reporting burden, and for capturing information on the CMS 416 relating to children's receipt of treatment services for which they are referred.
Oral Health: Efforts Under Way to Improve Children's Access to Dental Services, but Sustained Attention Needed to Address Ongoing Concerns. GAO-11-96, November 30, 2010	HHS should 1. establish a process to periodically verify that the dentist lists posted by states on the Insure Kids Now website are complete, usable, and accurate, and ensure that states and participating dentists have a common understanding of what it means for a dentist to indicate he or she can treat children with special needs; and 2. require states to verify that dentists listed on the Insure Kids Now website have not been excluded from Medicaid and the State Children's Health Insurance Program by the HHS Office of Inspector General, and periodically verify that excluded providers are not included on the lists posted by the states.

Medicaid: Key Issues Facing the Program

GAO Report	Open Recommendation
Medicaid: State and Federal Actions Have Been Taken to Improve Children's Access to Dental Services, but Gaps Remain. GAO-09-723, September 30, 2009	CMS should ensure that states found to have inadequate MCO dental provider networks take action to strengthen these networks.
Ensuring Fiscal Accountability through Increased Transparency and Improved Oversight	
Medicaid Demonstrations: Approval Criteria and Documentation Need to Show How Spending Furthers Medicaid Objectives. GAO-15-239, April 13, 2015	HHS should 1. issue criteria for assessing whether section 1115 expenditure authorities are likely to promote Medicaid objectives; 2. ensure the application of these criteria is documented in all HHS's approvals of section 1115 demonstrations, including those approving new or extending or modifying existing expenditure authorities, to inform internaland external stakeholders—including states, the public, and Congress—of the basis for the agency's determinations that approved expenditure authorities are likely to promote Medicaid objectives; 3. take steps to ensure that Medicaid demonstration approval documentation consistently provides assurances—such as through claiming protocols or the application template—that states will avoid duplicative spending by offsetting as appropriate all other federal revenues received when claiming federal Medicaid matching funds.
Medicaid: CMS Oversight of Provider Payments Is Hampered by Limited Data and Unclear Policy. GAO-15-322, April 10, 2015	CMS should 1. take steps to ensure that states report accurate provider specific payment data that include accurate unique national provider identifiers; 2. develop a policy establishing criteria for when such payments at the provider level are economical and efficient; and

66 United States Government Accountability Office

Table 4. (Continued)

GAO Report	Open Recommendation
	3. once criteria are developed, develop a process for identifying and reviewing payments to individual providers in order to determine whether they are economical and efficient.
Medicaid Financing: States' Increased Reliance on Funds from Health Care Providers and Local Governments Warrants Improved CMS Data Collection. GAO-14-627, July 29, 2014	CMS should develop a data collection strategy that ensures that states report accurate and complete data on all sources of funds used to finance the nonfederal share of Medicaid payments.
Medicaid Demonstration Waivers: Approval Process Raises Cost Concerns and Lacks Transparency. GAO-13-384, June 25, 2013	HHS should update the agency's written budget neutrality policy to reflect actualcriteria and processes used to develop and approve demonstration spending limits, and ensure the policy is readily available to state Medicaid directors and others.
Medicaid: CMS Needs More Information on the Billions of Dollars Spent on Supplemental Payments. GAO-08-614, May 30, 2008	CMS should develop a strategy to identify all of the supplemental payment programs established in states' Medicaid plans, and to review those programs that have not been subject to review under CMS's August 2003 initiative.
Medicaid Financing: Federal Oversight Initiative Is Consistent with Medicaid Payment Principles but Needs Greater Transparency. GAO-07-214, March 30, 2007	CMS should provide each state CMS reviews under its initiative to end inappropriate state financing arrangements with specific and written explanations regarding agency determinations on the allowability of various arrangements for financing the nonfederal share of Medicaid payments, and make these determinations available to all states and interested parties.
Improving Program Integrity	
Medicaid: Additional Actions Needed to Help Improve Provider and Beneficiary Fraud Controls. GAO-15-313, May 14, 2015	CMS should 1. issue guidance to states to better identify beneficiaries who are deceased; and

Medicaid: Key Issues Facing the Program

GAO Report	Open Recommendation
	2. provide guidance to states on the availability of automated information through Medicare's enrollment database—the Provider Enrollment, Chain, and Ownership System (PECOS)—and full access to all pertinent PECOS information, such as ownership information, to help screen Medicaid providers more efficiently and effectively.
Medicaid Information Technology: CMS Supports Use of Program Integrity Systems but Should Require States to Determine Effectiveness. GAO-15-207, January 30, 2015	HHS should direct CMS to require states to measure quantifiable benefits, such as cost reductions or avoidance, achieved as a result of operating information systems to help prevent and detect improper payments.
Medicaid: Additional Federal Action Needed to Further Improve Third-Party Liability Efforts. GAO-15-208, January 28, 2015	HHS should direct CMS to 1. routinely monitor and share across all states information regarding key third-party liability efforts and challenges; and 2. provide guidance to states on their oversight of third-party liability efforts conducted by Medicaid managed care plans.
Medicaid Program Integrity: Increased Oversight Needed to Ensure Integrity of Growing Managed Care Expenditures. GAO-14-341, May 19, 2014	CMS should 1. hold states accountable for Medicaid managed care program integrity by requiring states to conduct audits of payments to and by managed care organizations; and 2. update CMS's Medicaid managed care guidance on program integrity practices and effective handling of MCO recoveries.
Medicaid Integrity Program: CMS Should Take Steps to Eliminate Duplication and Improve Efficiency. GAO-13-50, November 13, 2012	CMS should reevaluate the agency's methodology for calculating a return on investment for the Medicaid Integrity Program and share its methodology withCongress and the states.
Fraud Detection Systems: Centers for Medicare and Medicaid Services Needs to Ensure More Widespread Use. GAO-11-475, June 30, 2011	CMS should implement and manage plans for incorporating data into the Integrated Data Repository to meet schedule milestones.

Source: GAO. | GAO-15-677

Appendix II: Selected Characteristics of States' Medicaid Programs

State	Regular FMAP rate in 2015[a]	Medicaid enrollment in 2012[b]	Medicaid benefit spending in 2014[c]	Percentage of enrollees in comprehensive risk-based managed care in 2011[d]	Whether the state had expanded Medicaid coverage to newly eligible adults under PPACA as of May 2015
Alabama	68.99	942,550	$5,213,247,879	3.1	No
Alaska	50.00	110,460	$1,412,407,094	0	No
Arizona	68.46	1,362,557[e]	$9,184,808,597	86.3	Yes
Arkansas	70.88	594,105	$4,840,075,746	Less than 0.05	Yes
California	50.00	9,474,835	$63,383,947,702	40.8	Yes
Colorado	51.01	650,857	$5,919,113,049	12.7	Yes
Connecticut	50.00	694,673	$6,820,658,024	59.2	Yes
Delaware	53.63	209,225	$1,691,771,386	78.5	Yes
District of Columbia	70.00	104,495	$2,367,792,161	72.4	Yes
Florida	59.72	3,248,265	$20,303,199,078	71.0	No
Georgia	66.94	1,243,109e	$9,396,958,654	68.8	No
Hawaii	52.23	249,392	$1,949,895,249	95.3	Yes
Idaho	71.75	222,767	$1,585,631,105	0	No
Illinois	50.76	2,672,129	$16,616,392,364	7.7	Yes
Indiana	66.52	1,007,151	$9,094,042,848	71.2	Yes
Iowa	55.54	498,659	$3,921,556,276	Less than 0.05	Yes
Kansas	56.63	349,499	$2,727,710,336	57.0	No

State	Regular FMAP rate in 2015[a]	Medicaid enrollment in 2012[b]	Medicaid benefit spending in 2014[c]	Percentage of enrollees in comprehensive risk-based managed care in 2011[d]	Whether the state had expanded Medicaid coverage to newly eligible adults under PPACA as of May 2015
Kentucky	69.94	769,622	$7,792,776,771	17.7	Yes
Louisiana	62.05	1,113,642	$7,055,593,669	Less than 0.05	No
Maine	61.88	370,562	$2,365,417,230	[f]	No
Maryland	50.00	926,611	$9,210,329,395	73.4	Yes
Massachusetts	50.00	1,080,050	$14,250,839,665	50.2	Yes
Michigan	65.54	1,885,402	$13,502,617,518	71.7	Yes
Minnesota	50.00	889,011	$9,917,891,767	68.4	Yes
Mississippi	73.58	654,811	$4,865,309,235	9.2	No
Missouri	63.45	931,450	$8,828,757,766	44.5	No
Montana	65.90	108,081	$1,072,160,721	0	Pending federal approval[g]
Nebraska	53.27	207,856	$1,771,909,070	45.0	No
Nevada	64.36	305,627	$2,281,105,301	57.6	Yes
New Hampshire	50.00	136,710	$1,322,700,772	0	Yes
New Jersey	50.00	971,261	$12,470,313,962	67.9	Yes
New Mexico	69.65	557,184	$4,168,980,357	67.0	Yes
New York	50.00	4,951,302	$51,806,022,238	66.9	Yes
North Carolina	65.88	1,619,903	$11,992,545,816	Less than 0.05	No
North Dakota	50.00	64,752	$401,980,406	2.3	Yes

(Continued)

State	Regular FMAP rate in 2015[a]	Medicaid enrollment in 2012[b]	Medicaid benefit spending in 2014[c]	Percentage of enrollees in comprehensive risk-based managed care in 2011[d]	Whether the state had expanded Medicaid coverage to newly eligible adults under PPACA as of May 2015
Ohio	62.64	2,105,533	$19,439,277,855	76.2	Yes
Oklahoma	62.30	723,119	$4,666,284,967	Less than 0.05	No
Oregon	64.06	617,726	$6,784,093,341	76.8	Yes
Pennsylvania	51.82	2,144,709	$23,461,728,946	60.0	Yes
Rhode Island	50.00	161,542	$2,436,946,880	60.0	Yes
South Carolina	70.64	852,904	$5,321,038,897	52.1	No
South Dakota	51.64	107,408	$778,125,953	0	No
Tennessee	64.99	1,321,683	$9,205,069,609	[f]	No
Texas	58.05	2,030,403e	$31,385,332,042	52.9	No
Utah	70.56	280,952	$2,064,362,848	3.4	No
Vermont	54.01	167,773	$1,526,126,311	[f]	Yes
Virginia	50.00	897,942	$7,547,405,238	60.5	No
Washington	50.03	1,157,897	$10,249,772,687	84.0	Yes
West Virginia	71.35	355,138	$3,331,020,307	52.8	Yes
Wisconsin	58.27	1,062,278	$7,396,295,700	80.4	No
Wyoming	50.00	68,458	$539,403,281	0	No

Source: GAO based on information from the Medicaid and CHIP Payment and Access Commission (MACPAC) (enrollment and spending data); Office of the Assistant Secretary for Planning and Evaluation, Department of Health and Human Services (regular FMAPs); and The Henry J. Kaiser Family Foundation (Medicaid expansion status). | GAO-15-677

[a] The federal government matches state Medicaid expenditures based on a statutory formula—the FMAP. The regular FMAP differs from the FMAP that may apply to certain individuals, such as those newly eligible for Medicaid under PPACA.

[b] Medicaid enrollment figures reflect full-year equivalent enrollment, which is the sum of monthly enrollment totals, divided by 12.

[c] Medicaid benefit spending figures include federal and state spending for 2014 as of February 25, 2015, and were subject to change if states revised their expenditure data.

[d] Comprehensive risk-based managed care plans do not include limited-benefit plans or primary care case management programs.

[e] State had a change in total enrollment of 10 percent or more over the prior year, which may reflect data anomalies and may be updated in the future.

[f] MACPAC did not report managed care information for Maine, Tennessee, or Vermont due to data issues.

[g] State enacted legislation expanding Medicaid; federal approval of the expansion is required before it can be implemented.

RELATED GAO PRODUCTS

The following are selected GAO products pertinent to the key issues discussed in this report. Other products may be found at GAO's web site at www.gao.gov.

Maintaining and Improving Access to Quality Care

Behavioral Health: Options for Low-Income Adults to Receive Treatment in Selected States. GAO-15-449. Washington, D.C.: June 19, 2015.

Medicaid: Service Utilization Patterns for Beneficiaries in Managed Care. GAO-15-481. Washington, D.C.: May 29, 2015.

Children's Health Insurance Program: Effects on Coverage and Access, and Considerations for Extending Funding. GAO-15-348. Washington, D.C.: February 27, 2015.

Foster Children: Additional Federal Guidance Could Help States Better Plan for Oversight of Psychotropic Medications Administered by Managed-Care Organizations. GAO-14-362. Washington, D.C.: April 28, 2014.

Children's Health Insurance: Information on Coverage of Services, Costs to Consumers, and Access to Care in CHIP and Other Sources of Insurance. GAO-14-40. Washington, D.C.: November 21, 2013.

Dental Services: Information on Coverage, Payments, and Fee Variation. GAO-13-754. Washington, D.C.: September 6, 2013.

Children's Mental Health: Concerns Remain about Appropriate Services for Children in Medicaid and Foster Care. GAO-13-15. Washington, D.C.: December 10, 2012.

Medicaid: States Made Multiple Program Changes, and Beneficiaries Generally Reported Access Comparable to Private Insurance. GAO-13-55. Washington, D.C.: November 15, 2012.

Foster Children: HHS Guidance Could Help States Improve Oversight of Psychotropic Prescriptions. GAO-12-201. Washington, D.C.: December 14, 2011.

Medicaid and CHIP: Most Physicians Serve Covered Children but Have Difficulty Referring Them for Specialty Care. GAO-11-624. Washington, D.C.: June 30, 2011.

Medicaid and CHIP: Reports for Monitoring Children's Health Care Services Need Improvement. GAO-11-293R. Washington, D.C.: April 5, 2011.

Medicaid and CHIP: Given the Association between Parent and Child Insurance Status, New Expansions May Benefit Families. GAO-11-264. Washington, D.C.: February 4, 2011.

Oral Health: Efforts Under Way to Improve Children's Access to Dental Services, but Sustained Attention Needed to Address Ongoing Concerns. GAO-11-96. Washington, D.C.: November 30, 2010.

Medicaid: State and Federal Actions Have Been Taken to Improve Children's Access to Dental Services, but Gaps Remain. GAO-09-723. Washington, D.C.: September 30, 2009.

Medicaid Preventive Services: Concerted Efforts Needed to Ensure Beneficiaries Receive Services. GAO-09-578. Washington, D.C.: August 14, 2009.

Medicaid: Extent of Dental Disease in Children Has Not Decreased, and Millions Are Estimated to Have Untreated Tooth Decay. GAO-08-1121. Washington, D.C.: September 23, 2008.

Medicaid: Concerns Remain about Sufficiency of Data for Oversight of Children's Dental Services. GAO-07-826T. Washington, D.C.: May 2, 2007.

Ensuring Fiscal Accountability through Increased Transparency and Improved Oversight

Medicaid Demonstrations: More Transparency and Accountability for Approved Spending Are Needed. GAO-15-715T. Washington, D.C.: June 24, 2015.

Medicaid Demonstrations: Approval Criteria and Documentation Need to Show How Spending Furthers Medicaid Objectives. GAO-15-239. Washington, D.C.: April 13, 2015.

Medicaid: CMS Oversight of Provider Payments Is Hampered by Limited Data and Unclear Policy. GAO-15-322. Washington, D.C.: April 10, 2015.

Medicaid Financing: Questionnaire Data on States' Methods for Financing Medicaid Payments from 2008 through 2012. GAO-15-227SP. Washington, D.C.: March 13, 2015, an e-supplement to GAO-14-627.

Medicaid Demonstrations: HHS's Approval Process for Arkansas's Medicaid Expansion Waiver Raises Cost Concerns. GAO-14-689R. Washington, D.C.: August 8, 2014.

74 United States Government Accountability Office

Medicaid: Completed and Preliminary Work Indicate that Transparency around State Financing Methods and Payments to Providers Is Still Needed for Oversight. GAO-14-817T. Washington, D.C.: July 29, 2014.

Medicaid Financing: States' Increased Reliance on Funds from Health Care Providers and Local Governments Warrants Improved CMS Data Collection. GAO-14-627. Washington, D.C.: July 29, 2014.

Medicaid Demonstration Waivers: Approval Process Raises Cost Concerns and Lacks Transparency. GAO-13-384. Washington, D.C.: June 25, 2013.

Medicaid: More Transparency of and Accountability for Supplemental Payments Are Needed. GAO-13-48. Washington, D.C.: November 26, 2012.

Medicaid: Data Sets Provide Inconsistent Picture of Expenditures. GAO-13-47. Washington, D.C.: October 29, 2012.

Medicaid: States Reported Billions More in Supplemental Payments in Recent Years. GAO-12-694. Washington, D.C.: July 20, 2012.

Medicaid: Ongoing Federal Oversight of Payments to Offset Uncompensated Hospital Care Costs Is Warranted. GAO-10-69. Washington, D.C.: November 20, 2009.

Medicaid: CMS Needs More Information on the Billions of Dollars Spent on Supplemental Payments. GAO-08-614. Washington, D.C.: May 30, 2008.

Medicaid Financing: Long-standing Concerns about Inappropriate State Arrangements Support Need for Improved Federal Oversight. GAO-08-650T. Washington, D.C.: April 3, 2008.

Medicaid Demonstration Waivers: Recent HHS Approvals Continue to Raise Cost and Oversight Concerns. GAO-08-87. Washington, D.C.: January 31, 2008.

Medicaid Financing: Long-Standing Concerns about Inappropriate State Arrangements Support Need for Improved Federal Oversight. GAO-08-255T. Washington, D.C.: November 1, 2007.

Medicaid Demonstration Waivers: Lack of Opportunity for Public Input during Federal Approval Process Still a Concern. GAO-07-694R. Washington, D.C.: July 24, 2007.

Medicaid Financing: Federal Oversight Initiative Is Consistent with Medicaid Payment Principles but Needs Greater Transparency. GAO-07-214. Washington, D.C.: March 30, 2007.

Medicaid and SCHIP: Recent HHS Approvals of Demonstration Waiver Projects Raise Concerns. GAO-02-817. Washington, D.C.: July 12, 2002.

Improving Program Integrity

Medicaid: Additional Actions Needed to Help Improve Provider and Beneficiary Fraud Controls. GAO-15-313. Washington, D.C.: May 14, 2015.

Medicaid Information Technology: CMS Supports Use of Program Integrity Systems but Should Require States to Determine Effectiveness. GAO-15-207. Washington, D.C.: January 30, 2015.

Medicaid: Additional Federal Action Needed to Further Improve Third- Party Liability Efforts. GAO-15-208. Washington, D.C.: January 28, 2015.

Medicaid Program Integrity: Increased Oversight Needed to Ensure Integrity of Growing Managed Care Expenditures. GAO-14-341. Washington, D.C.: May 19, 2014.

Medicaid: CMS Should Ensure That States Clearly Report Overpayments. GAO-14-25. Washington, D.C.: December 6, 2013.

Medicaid: Enhancements Needed for Improper Payments Reporting and Related Corrective Action Monitoring. GAO-13-229. Washington, D.C.: March 29, 2013.

Medicaid Integrity Program: CMS Should Take Steps to Eliminate Duplication and Improve Efficiency. GAO-13-50. Washington, D.C.: November 13, 2012.

National Medicaid Audit Program: CMS Should Improve Reporting and Focus on Audit Collaboration with States. GAO-12-814T. Washington, D.C.: June, 14, 2012.

Program Integrity: Further Action Needed to Address Vulnerabilities in Medicaid and Medicare Programs. GAO-12-803T. Washington, D.C.: June 7, 2012.

Medicaid: Federal Oversight of Payments and Program Integrity Needs Improvement. GAO-12-674T. Washington, D.C.: April 25, 2012.

Medicaid Program Integrity: Expanded Federal Role Presents Challenges to and Opportunities for Assisting States. GAO-12-288T. Washington, D.C.: December 7, 2011.

Fraud Detection Systems: Centers for Medicare and Medicaid Services Needs to Expand Efforts to Support Program Integrity Initiatives. GAO-12-292T. Washington, D.C.: December 7, 2011.

Fraud Detection Systems: Centers for Medicare and Medicaid Services Needs to Ensure More Widespread Use. GAO-11-475. Washington, D.C.: June 30, 2011.

76 United States Government Accountability Office

Medicare and Medicaid Fraud, Waste, and Abuse: Effective Implementation of Recent Laws and Agency Actions Could Help Reduce Improper Payments. GAO-11-409T. Washington, D.C.: March 9, 2011.

Medicaid Managed Care: CMS's Oversight of States' Rate Setting Needs Improvement. GAO-10-810. Washington, D.C.: August 4, 2010.

Addressing Variations in States' Financing Needs Through Revised Federal Financing Approach

Medicaid: Alternative Measures Could Be Used to Allocate Funding More Equitably. GAO-13-434. Washington, D.C.: May 10, 2013.

Medicaid: Prototype Formula Would Provide Automatic, Targeted Assistance to States during Economic Downturns. GAO-12-38. Washington, D.C.: November 10, 2011.

Medicaid: Improving Responsiveness of Federal Assistance to States during Economic Downturns. GAO-11-395. Washington, D.C.: March 31, 2011.

State and Local Governments: Knowledge of Past Recessions Can Inform Future Federal Fiscal Assistance. GAO-11-401. Washington, D.C.: March 31, 2011.

Recovery Act: Increased Medicaid Funds Aided Enrollment Growth, and Most States Reported Taking Steps to Sustain Their Programs. GAO-11-58. Washington, D.C.: October 8, 2010.

Medicaid: Strategies to Help States Address Increased Expenditures during Economic Downturns. GAO-07-97. Washington, D.C.: October 18, 2006.

Federal Assistance: Temporary State Fiscal Relief. GAO-04-736R. Washington, D.C.: May 7, 2004.

Medicaid Formula: Differences in Funding Ability among States Often Are Widened. GAO-03-620. Washington, D.C.: July 10, 2003.

Other GAO Products

Medicaid: Overview of Key Issues Facing the Program. GAO-15-746T. Washington, D.C.: July 8, 2015.

Medicaid: A Small Share of Enrollees Consistently Accounted for a Large Share of Expenditures. GAO-15-460. Washington, D.C.: May 8, 2015

2015 Annual Report: Additional Opportunities to Reduce Fragmentation, Overlap, and Duplication and Achieve Other Financial Benefits. GAO-15-404SP. Washington, D.C.: April 14, 2015.

High-Risk Series: An Update. GAO-15-290. Washington, D.C.: February 11, 2015.

Medicaid: Federal Funds Aid Eligibility IT System Changes, but Implementation Challenges Persist. GAO-15-169. Washington, D.C.: December, 12, 2014.

Medicaid Payment: Comparisons of Selected Services under Fee-for- Service, Managed Care, and Private Insurance. GAO-14-533. Washington, D.C.: July 15, 2014.

Prescription Drugs: Comparison of DOD, Medicaid, and Medicare Part D Retail Reimbursement Prices. GAO-14-578. Washington, D.C.: June 30, 2014.

Medicaid: Assessment of Variation among States in Per-Enrollee Spending. GAO-14-456. Washington, D.C.: June 16, 2014.

Medicaid: Demographics and Service Usage of Certain High-Expenditure Beneficiaries. GAO-14-176. Washington, D.C.: February 19, 2014.

Medicaid: Use of Claims Data for Analysis of Provider Payment Rates. GAO-14-56R. Washington, D.C.: January 6, 2014.

Medicaid Managed Care: Use of Limited Benefit Plans to Provide Mental Health Services and Efforts to Coordinate Care. GAO-13-780. Washington, D.C.: September 30, 2013.

Medicaid: States' Use of Managed Care. GAO-12-872R. Washington, D.C.: August, 17, 2012.

Medicaid: States' Plans to Pursue New and Revised Options for Home- and Community-Based Services. GAO-12-649. Washington, D.C.: June 13, 2012.

Medicaid and CHIP: Enrollment, Benefits, Expenditures, and Other Characteristics of State Premium Assistance Programs. GAO-10-258R. Washington, D.C.: January 19, 2010.

End Notes

[1] Centers for Medicare & Medicaid Services, Office of the Actuary, *2014 Actuarial Report on the Financial Outlook for Medicaid* (Washington, D.C.: 2015).

[2] This figure represents the total number of individuals ever enrolled in the program in 2013. There were about 58 million individuals enrolled in the program at any one point in time. See Medicaid and CHIP Payment and Access Commission, *Report to the Congress on*

78 United States Government Accountability Office

Medicaid and CHIP (Washington, D.C.: March 2014). When presenting statistics regarding Medicaid, we have attempted to use the most recent and reliable data available; as a result, we present data from different years, for different purposes.

[3] CMS, *2014 Actuarial Report on the Financial Outlook for Medicaid.*

[4] See, for example, GAO, *High-Risk Series: An Update*, GAO-15-290 (Washington, D.C.: Feb. 11, 2015).

[5] Among these traditional enrollees, persons with disabilities and individuals age 65 and over may be enrolled in Medicare as well and are referred to as dual-eligible enrollees.

[6] Pub. L. No. 111-148, 124 Stat. 119 (2010), as amended by the Health Care and Education Reconciliation Act of 2010 (HCERA), Pub. L. No. 111-152, 124 Stat. 1029 (2010). For purposes of this report, references to PPACA include the amendments made by HCERA. Beginning in 2014, states may cover under their state plan non-elderly, non- pregnant adults with incomes at or below 133 percent of the FPL. PPACA also permitted an early expansion option, whereby states could expand eligibility for this population (or a subset of this population) starting April 1, 2010. Additionally, PPACA provides for a 5 percent disregard when calculating income for determining Medicaid eligibility for this population, which effectively increases this income level to 138 percent of the FPL. In this report, we refer to this population as "expansion enrollees."

[7] Some optional services—including, for example, personal care services for the frail elderly and individuals with disabilities who need LTSS, and adult dental care—are commonly covered. However, among states that offer a particular benefit, the breadth of coverage (i.e., amount, duration, and scope) of that benefit can vary greatly.

[8] Non-institutional LTSS include home health and personal care services, among other services.

[9] We examined expenditures among Medicaid-only enrollees. See GAO, *Medicaid: A Small Share of Enrollees Consistently Accounted for a Large Share of Expenditures*, GAO-15-460 (Washington, D.C.: May 8, 2015); and *Medicaid: Demographics and Service Usage of Certain High Expenditure Beneficiaries*, GAO-14-176 (Washington D.C.: Feb. 19, 2014).

[10] States must submit an application describing the proposed demonstration, and in some cases, the potential budgetary effect, for HHS approval.

[11] States submit their estimated expenditures on Form CMS-37 at least 45 days before the beginning of each fiscal quarter. States are to submit their actual expenditures on Form CMS-64 30 days after the end of each fiscal quarter.

[12] This state-expansion FMAP falls between a state's regular FMAP and the PPACA- expansion FMAP.

[13] See GAO, *Medicaid: States Made Multiple Program Changes, and Beneficiaries Generally Reported Access Comparable to Private Insurance*, GAO-13-55 (Washington, D.C.: Nov. 15, 2012).

[14] See GAO, *Children's Health Insurance: Information on Coverage of Services, Costs to Consumers, and Access to Care in CHIP and Other Sources of Insurance*, GAO-14-40 (Washington, D.C.: Nov. 21, 2013).

[15] See GAO-13-55.

[16] Federal law historically has not required states to cover preventive services for adults in Medicaid and coverage of these services and access to them has varied across the states. PPACA required states to cover certain recommended preventive services for newly eligible adults in states that expand coverage under the law; preventive services for adults in Medicaid continue to be an optional benefit otherwise, but PPACA provides incentives for states to cover them. See GAO, *Medicaid Preventive Services: Concerted Efforts Needed to Ensure Beneficiaries Receive Services*, GAO-09-578 (Washington, D.C.: Aug. 14, 2009); and *High-Risk Series: An Update*, GAO-15-290 (Washington, D.C: Feb. 11, 2015).

[17] We surveyed officials in 2012 and asked about their experiences from 2008 through 2011. See GAO-13-55.

Medicaid: Key Issues Facing the Program 79

[18] See GAO-14-40. For other findings about children's health care, see GAO, *Medicaid and CHIP: Reports for Monitoring Children's Health Care Services Need Improvement*, GAO-11-293R (Washington, D.C.: April 5, 2011).

[19] Our survey asked physicians about both children covered by Medicaid and the State Children's Health Insurance Program (CHIP), a joint federal-state program that provides health coverage to certain low-income children. In reporting our results, we did not report separate information for Medicaid- and CHIP-covered children. For the purposes of this report, we refer to those survey findings as applying to Medicaid-covered children, who account for the majority of all children who are covered by either program. See GAO, *Medicaid and CHIP: Most Physicians Serve Covered Children but Have Difficulty Referring Them for Specialty Care*, GAO-11-624 (Washington, D.C.: June 30, 2011).

[20] See Substance Abuse and Mental Health Services Administration, *Results from the 2013 National Survey on Drug Use and Health: Mental Health Findings*, NSDUH Series H-49, HHS Publication No. (SMA) 14-4887. (Rockville, Md.: November 2014).

[21] GAO, *Behavioral Health: Options for Low-Income Adults to Receive Treatment in Selected States*, GAO-15-449 (Washington, D.C.: June 19, 2015).

[22] See GAO-13-55.

[23] For example, over 80 percent did not receive any psychosocial therapy and 70 percent did not have any mental health office visits. While this was also true for privately-insured children, the percentage of such children who had a potential need for mental health services was lower than among Medicaid-covered children (9 percent versus 14 percent). See GAO, *Children's Mental Health: Concerns Remain about Appropriate Services for Children in Medicaid and Foster Care*, GAO-13-15 (Washington, D.C.: Dec. 10, 2012).

[24] Nearly two-thirds of Medicaid-covered children who took psychotropic medication did not receive psychosocial therapy or counseling, and one-fourth did not have any mental health-related office visit, suggesting they did not have a medication-management follow- up visit, which pediatric provider organizations recommend. While not all children would necessarily benefit from both medication and therapy, the American Academy of Child & Adolescent Psychiatry has stated that medication alone is rarely adequate treatment for children with complex mental health needs.

[25] In December 2011, we reported that Medicaid-covered children in foster care in selected states were prescribed psychotropic medications at higher rates than nonfoster children in Medicaid during 2008. In 2012, HHS's Administration for Children and Families issued guidance to state agencies seeking to improve their monitoring and oversight practices for psychotropic medications. See GAO, *Foster Children: Additional Federal Guidance Could Help States Better Plan for Oversight of Psychotropic Medications Administered by Managed-Care Organizations*, GAO-14-362 (Washington, D.C.: April 28, 2014); and *Foster Children: HHS Guidance Could Help States Improve Oversight of Psychotropic Prescriptions*, GAO-12-201 (Washington, D.C.: Dec. 14, 2011).

[26] See GAO-14-362.

[27] See GAO, *Dental Services: Information on Coverage, Payments, and Fee Variation*, GAO-13-754 (Washington, D.C.: Sept. 6, 2013).

[28] See GAO, *Extent of Dental Disease in Children Has Not Decreased, and Millions Are Estimated to Have Untreated Tooth Decay*, GAO-08-1121 (Washington, D.C.: Sept. 23, 2008).

[29] See GAO-13-55.

[30] See GAO, *Oral Health: Efforts Under Way to Improve Children's Access to Dental Services, but Sustained Attention Needed to Address Ongoing Concerns*, GAO-11-96 (Washington, D.C.: Nov. 30, 2010); and *Medicaid: State and Federal Actions Have Been Taken to Improve Children's Access to Dental Services, but Gaps Remain*, GAO-09-723 (Washington, D.C.: Sept. 30, 2009).

[31] HHS is required to exclude individuals and entities convicted of certain criminal offenses, including Medicare or Medicaid fraud. HHS may also exclude individuals and entities for

80 United States Government Accountability Office

certain offenses, including license revocation or default on Health Education Assistance Loans. The HHS Office of Inspector General (OIG) administers the HHS exclusion program. See GAO-11-96.

[32] CMS officials noted in March 2015 that it is not possible for them to reliably determine whether providers listed on the HHS OIG's list of excluded providers match any of the dentists submitted by states to the Insure Kids Now website because the website data does not include provider identification numbers, only provider names. CMS officials noted that, during oral health-related meetings with states, agency officials would ask whether states are removing excluded providers when they submit updated information for the Insure Kids Now website.

[33] See GAO-09-723.

[34] Under federal law, the EPSDT benefit generally entitles children in Medicaid to receive coverage of periodic screening services—often termed well-child checkups—that include a comprehensive health and developmental history, a comprehensive physical exam, appropriate immunizations, laboratory tests, and health education.

[35] For example, CMS uses these reports to monitor states' progress in meeting the agency's annual goal that states provide a well-child check-up to at least 80 percent of the children eligible to receive one. We have previously found that a significant number of children in Medicaid may not be receiving basic preventive care. For example, we found in 2009 that, on the basis of parents' reports in national surveys conducted by HHS from 2003 through 2006, about 40 percent of children in Medicaid and CHIP had not had a well-child checkup over a 2-year period. See GAO-09-578.

[36] See GAO, Children's Health Insurance Program: Effects on Coverage and Access, and Considerations for Extending Funding, GAO-15-348 (Washington, D.C.: Feb. 27, 2015).

[37] Few states met CMS's goal of providing a well-child checkup to at least 80 percent of children eligible to receive one. See GAO-11-293R.

[38] See GAO-11-293R.

[39] See GAO-15-348.

[40] Although states have submitted data on managed care utilization—also known as encounter data—to CMS since 1999, these encounter data have historically been relatively incomplete and unreliable. Recent evidence suggests that the quality of Medicaid encounter data may be improving. See GAO, Medicaid: Service Utilization Patterns for Beneficiaries in Managed Care, GAO-15-481 (Washington, D.C.: May 29, 2015).

[41] See http://www.gao.gov/products/GAO-15-481 for the percentage of adult enrollees in each state who used at least one professional service and for the number of services they used.

[42] States' regular Medicaid payments are not required to fully cover the costs of providing Medicaid services.

[43] States are required by federal law to make DSH payments to certain hospitals. These payments are designed to help offset these hospitals' uncompensated care costs for serving large numbers of Medicaid and uninsured individuals. Under Medicaid rules, states can obtain federal matching funds for payments made under the UPL, which is based on the amount Medicare would pay for comparable services as applied to all providers within specified ownership classes. Medicaid UPL supplemental payments, which are above the regular Medicaid payments but within the UPL, are not limited to an individual provider's cost of providing Medicaid services. States may also make supplemental payments to hospitals, nursing facilities, and other providers under Medicaid demonstrations.

[44] Under federal law, to receive federal matching funds, payments generally (1) must be made for covered Medicaid items and services; (2) must be consistent with economy, efficiency, and quality of care; and (3) must not exceed the Medicaid UPL.

[45] In recent years, states have reported increasing amounts of Medicaid UPL supplemental payments, which first exceeded DSH payments in fiscal year 2011, when Medicaid UPL supplemental payments totaled nearly $26 billion compared to over $17 billion for DSH payments. See GAO, Medicaid: States Reported Billions More in Supplemental Payments

in Recent Years, GAO-12-694 (Washington, D.C.: July 20, 2012); and *Medicaid: More Transparency of and Accountability for Supplemental Payments Are Needed*, GAO-13-48 (Washington, D.C.: Nov. 26, 2012).

[46] See GAO, *Medicaid: CMS Oversight of Provider Payments Is Hampered by Limited Data and Unclear Policy*, GAO-15-322 (Washington, D.C.: April 10, 2015).

[47] Of the 505 hospitals, 310 received a supplemental payment that, when added to the regular Medicaid payments the hospital received, resulted in total Medicaid payments exceeding Medicaid costs by about $1.9 billion. The remaining 195 hospitals received regular Medicaid payments that exceeded Medicaid costs before they received a supplemental payment, and total payments exceeded costs by about $900 million. See GAO-13-48.

[48] Average daily payments to government hospitals were comparable to those made to private hospitals in one state, and somewhat higher for government providers in a second state, but these averages masked wide variation in the daily payment amounts that the two states were paying individual providers. See GAO-15-322.

[49] See GAO-15-322.

[50] For the CMS-64 data set, states are required to submit their aggregate total quarterly Medicaid expenditures via a form CMS-64, which CMS uses to determine the amount of federal matching funds to provide to states for these expenditures. CMS reviews the states' submissions, and the data are the most-reliable accounting of total Medicaid expenditures. However, CMS-64 data exclude enrollee-specific data and thus are of limited use for examining program spending. MSIS was established as a national eligibility and claims data set, and can provide CMS a summary of expenditures linked to specific enrollees on the basis of their medical claims for care. For MSIS, states are required to submit to CMS quarterly electronic files that contain (1) information on people covered by Medicaid, and (2) adjudicated claims for medical services reimbursed by Medicaid. CMS reviews these data for reliability, and uses these data for policy analysis, program utilization, and forecasting expenditures. However, these data exclude other aspects of the Medicaid program that are not tied to specific enrollees.

[51] See GAO, *Medicaid: Data Sets Provide Inconsistent Picture of Expenditures*, GAO-13-47 (Washington, D.C.: Oct. 29, 2012).

[52] These requirements, which were mandated by statute, include a provision requiring states to include in their annual DSH reports facility-specific information on the costs of serving Medicaid and uninsured patients and payments received from or on behalf of these patients.

[53] See GAO-15-322 and GAO, *Medicaid Financing: States' Increased Reliance on Funds from Health Care Providers and Local Governments Warrants Improved CMS Data Collection*, GAO-14-627 (Washington, D.C.: July 29, 2014).

[54] See GAO-15-322.

[55] See GAO-15-322.

[56] See GAO-13-48.

[57] See GAO-15-322 and GAO-14-627.

[58] See GAO-15-322. In addition, in 2008, we recommended that CMS develop a strategy to identify all of the supplemental payment programs established in states' Medicaid plans and to review those programs that had not been subject to review under a related CMS initiative. See GAO, *Medicaid: CMS Needs More Information on the Billions of Dollars Spent on Supplemental Payments*, GAO-08-614 (Washington, D.C.: May 30, 2008).

In 2012, CMS stated that it was undertaking a comprehensive review of all approved state plan amendments to scrutinize supplemental payment methodologies. CMS reported that, as part of this effort, it would identify states that are failing to report supplemental payments as required, and would address methodologies that do not comply with the Medicaid statute and federal regulation. This analysis would assist CMS in determining the need for more guidance or definitions of formulas, data sources, validation, and updates related to state UPL calculations and payments. See GAO-13-48. In March 2015, CMS officials said the agency was studying the results of this review.

[59] States finance their share of Medicaid, in large part, through state general funds, and are allowed to use other funding sources, such as taxes on health care providers and funds transfers from local governments, to finance the remainder.

[60] The requirement to finance at least 40 percent of the nonfederal share is applied in the aggregate and not for specific payments or payment arrangements.

[61] See GAO-14-627.

[62] The percentage and amount of funds from health care providers and local governments that states used to finance the nonfederal share of Medicaid payments varied significantly among states in state fiscal year 2012. For example, in the 48 states that reported using funds from health care providers and local governments, the percentage of funds from providers and local governments ranged from less than 1 percent in South Dakota and Virginia to 53 percent in Missouri. See GAO-14-627.

[63] See GAO-14-627.

[64] HHS acknowledged that it does not have adequate data on state financing methods for overseeing compliance with a certain federal requirement related to the nonfederal share— the 60 percent limit on contributions from local governments to finance the nonfederal share—and stated that it will examine efforts to improve data collection toward this end. HHS also stated that it is working to identify needs for improvement in current payment and financing review processes. However, HHS did not concur with two options our recommendation suggested for short- and long-term ways of improving agency data collection. Specifically, HHS disagreed with suggestions that facility-specific data are needed for oversight, and that T-MSIS may be an appropriate means for collecting financing data. HHS believes that its current financing reviews are sufficiently reviewing provider-level data. See GAO-14-627.

[65] 42 U.S.C. § 1315(a).

[66] Calculation is based on expenditures for medical assistance payments only, which for fiscal year 2014 were $146.8 billion for section 1115 demonstrations and $466.5 billion for total Medicaid expenditures, as reported in the Medicaid Budget and Expenditure System, as of January 2015.

[67] HHS's budget neutrality policy requires states to show that their demonstrations will be budget neutral as part of their application to HHS. HHS has implemented a budget neutrality policy for section 1115 demonstrations since the 1980's. The most recent version of this policy was published in 2001.

[68] See, for example, GAO, *Medicaid Demonstrations: HHS's Approval Process for Arkansas's Medicaid Expansion Waiver Raises Cost Concerns,* GAO-14-689R (Washington, D.C.: Aug. 8, 2014); *Medicaid Demonstration Waivers: Approval Process Raises Cost Concerns and Lacks Transparency,* GAO-13-384 (Washington, D.C.: June 25, 2013); *Medicaid Demonstration Waivers: Recent HHS Approvals Continue to Raise Cost and Oversight Concerns,* GAO-08-87 (Washington, D.C.: Jan. 31, 2008); and *Medicaid and SCHIP: Recent HHS Approvals of Demonstration Waiver Projects Raise Concerns,* GAO-02-817 (Washington, D.C.: July 12, 2002).

[69] According to HHS's policy, a state's demonstration spending limit should be based on the projected cost of continuing the state's existing Medicaid program without the proposed demonstration, as determined by two factors: (1) the spending baseline for the population covered by the demonstration, and (2) a spending growth rate. HHS has guidelines and benchmarks for spending baselines and growth rates. For example, spending baselines must exclude certain expenditures, and growth rates must be based on the lower of: (1) the state's historical growth for Medicaid in recent years, or (2) the President's budget Medicaid trend rate projected for the nation. Some types of section 1115 demonstrations, such as those that redirect a state's DSH funding, are not required to follow this process for determining spending limits. For details on HHS's policy and the process for determining budget neutrality, see GAO-13-384.

Medicaid: Key Issues Facing the Program   83

[70] In this state, the spending baseline included hypothetical costs that represented higher payments that the state could have paid for inpatient hospital services, rather than the actual amount of payments the state made. HHS also allowed one state to include projected costs rather than actual expenditures in its spending baseline. In addition, for 4 of 10 demonstrations we reviewed, HHS approved spending limits that were based on assumptions of cost growth that were higher than those reflected by the state's historical spending and the President's budget. See GAO-13-384.

[71] See GAO-14-689R.

[72] The 11 states other than Arkansas are Arizona, California, Iowa, Massachusetts, Michigan, New Jersey, New Mexico, New York, Oregon, Rhode Island, and Vermont. See GAO-14-689R.

[73] See GAO-13-384.

[74] PPACA required the Secretary of HHS to issue regulations for section 1115 applications and extensions that address certain topics including a state and federal public notice and comment process, submission of reports on implementation by states, and periodic evaluation by HHS. In response, on February 27, 2012, HHS published final regulations establishing these requirements for new section 1115 Medicaid demonstration applications and extensions. Pub. L. No. 111-148, § 10201, 124 Stat.119, 922 (2010); 77 Fed. Reg. 11,678 (Feb. 27, 2012).

[75] See GAO, *Medicaid Demonstrations: Approval Criteria and Documentation Need to Show How Spending Furthers Medicaid Objectives*, GAO-15-239 (Washington, D.C.: April 13, 2015).

[76] The state programs were wide-ranging in nature and included those providing health services, insurance subsidies, and workforce training. For example, one program constructs supportive housing for the homeless and another program recruits and aims to retain health care workers.

[77] See GAO-15-239.

[78] See GAO-15-290.

[79] CMS reported that the Medicaid improper payment rate increased from 5.8 percent for fiscal year 2013 to 6.7 percent for fiscal year 2014. The improper payment rate is a composite of different types of improper payment rates, including fee-for-service and managed care payments, and both active and negative eligibility determinations—that is, both individuals who were determined to be eligible and those determined to be ineligible and thus denied enrollment. For fiscal year 2014, CMS reported an error rate of 5.1 percent for fee-for-service payments, 0.2 percent for managed care payments, and 3.1 percent for eligibility determinations. Within the Medicaid eligibility case error rate, the active case error rate is 2.8 percent and the negative case error rate is 4.8 percent.

[80] See GAO, *Medicaid Program Integrity: Increased Oversight Needed to Ensure Integrity of Growing Managed Care Expenditures*, GAO-14-341 (Washington, D.C.: May 19, 2014).

[81] 80 Fed. Reg. 31098 (June 1, 2015).

[82] See GAO, *Medicaid Information Technology: CMS Supports Use of Program Integrity Systems but Should Require States to Determine Effectiveness*, GAO-15-207 (Washington, D.C.: Jan. 30, 2015).

[83] See GAO, *Medicaid Integrity Program: CMS Should Take Steps to Eliminate Duplication and Improve Efficiency*, GAO-13-50 (Washington, D.C.: Nov. 13, 2012).

[84] See GAO-13-50.

[85] See GAO, *Medicaid: Additional Federal Action Needed to Further ImproveThird-Party Liability Efforts*, GAO-15-208 (Washington, D.C.: Jan. 28, 2015).

[86] One such safeguard included in federal law is the requirement that states' capitation rates be actuarially sound. CMS regulations issued in 2002 define actuarially sound rates as those that are (1) developed in accordance with generally accepted actuarial principles and practices; (2) appropriate for the populations to be covered and the services to be furnished; and (3) certified as meeting applicable regulatory requirements by qualified actuaries. The

84 United States Government Accountability Office

regulations also specify the documentation states are required to submit to CMS to demonstrate compliance with the requirements, including a description of their rate-setting methodology and the data used to set rates. See 42 C.F.R. § 438.6(c)(1)(i)(2014).

[87] See GAO, *Medicaid Managed Care: CMS's Oversight of States' Rate Setting Needs Improvement*, GAO-10-810 (Washington, D.C.: Aug. 4, 2010).

[88] The federal government can exclude health care providers from participating in the Medicaid program for several reasons, including criminal convictions related to Medicare or state health programs, or other major problems related to health care (e.g., patient abuse or neglect). Excluded providers can be placed on one or both of the following exclusion lists, which Medicaid officials must check before paying for a claim: the List of Excluded Individuals/Entities, managed by HHS, and the System for Award Management, managed by the General Services Administration.

[89] See GAO, *Medicaid: Additional Actions Needed to Help Improve Provider and Beneficiary Fraud Controls*, GAO-15-313 (Washington, D.C.: May 14, 2015).

[90] For example, individuals' Medicaid applications may have inaccuracies due to simple errors, such as inaccurate data entry, making it difficult to determine whether these cases involve improper payments or fraud through data matching alone. In addition, there may be situations where an individual does not have a Social Security number (for example, a newborn child).

[91] Under federal regulations, enrollees are not to have payments made on their behalf by two or more states concurrently. In some instances, an enrollee may obtain services in a different state, but his or her resident state should pay for the eligible services.

[92] See GAO-15-313.

[93] The Data Services Hub verifies application information using various external data sources, such as the Social Security Administration and the Department of Homeland Security. According to CMS, the hub can verify key application information, including household income, state residency, and incarceration status.

[94] Officials at the four states we examined said that they periodically check the state vital records to determine whether a potential Medicaid beneficiary has died, but that they did not use a more-comprehensive Social Security Administration data source to perform this check outside of the initial enrollment or annual revalidation period. As a result, states may not be able to detect individuals who have moved to and died in other states. We also found that none of the four states were using a Medicare enrollment database to screen their entire provider population, and that additional CMS guidance to the states on requesting automated information through this database could help states improve efficiency of provider screening.

[95] See GAO, *Medicaid: Improving Responsiveness of Federal Assistance to States during Economic Downturns*, GAO-11-395 (Washington, D.C.: March 31, 2011).

[96] Pub. L. No. 108-27, § 401(a), 117 Stat. 752, 764 (2003). States were protected against decreases in their regular FMAP and could be eligible for an increased FMAP from April 1, 2003, through June 30, 2004.

[97] Pub. L. No. 111-5, Div. B, Tit. V, § 5001, 123 Stat. 115, 496 (2009). Congress subsequently extended this funding, which resulted in states receiving an estimated $16.1 billion in additional FMAP assistance. See Pub. L. No. 111-226, Tit. II, Subtit. A, § 201, 124 Stat. 2389, 2393 (2010).

[98] See GAO-11-395 and GAO, *State and Local Governments: Knowledge of Past Recessions Can Inform Future Federal Fiscal Assistance*, GAO-11-401 (Washington, D.C.: March 31, 2011); and *Federal Assistance: Temporary State Fiscal Relief*, GAO-04-736R (Washington, D.C.: May 7, 2004).

[99] See GAO-11-395 and GAO *Medicaid: Prototype Formula Would Provide Automatic, Targeted Assistance to States during Economic Downturns*; GAO-12-38 (Washington, D.C.: Nov. 10, 2011).

Medicaid: Key Issues Facing the Program 85

[100] For example, we found that after the 2001 and 2007 recessions ended, Medicaid enrollment remained high or increased in most states, even as revenues continued to decrease or remain below their prerecession levels. Congress later provided an extension to phase out the increased FMAPs from January through June 2011, which eased states' transition back to their regular FMAPs.

[101] See GAO-12-38.

[102] The employment-to-population ratio compares the number of employed persons in a state to the working age population aged 16 and older.

[103] See, for example, GAO, *Older Americans Act: Options to Better Target Need and Improve Equity*, GAO-13-74 (Washington, D.C.: Nov. 30, 2012); and *Changing Medicaid Formula Can Improve Distribution of Funds to States*, GAO/GGD-83-27 (Washington, D.C.: March 9, 1983).

[104] See, for example, GAO, *Medicaid Formula: Differences in Funding Ability among States Often Are Widened*, GAO-03-620 (Washington, D.C.: July 10, 2003).

[105] We reported in 2003 that, for example, the District of Columbia and Connecticut had similar per capita incomes, but the share of the District's population in poverty was more than twice Connecticut's. See GAO-03-620.

[106] See GAO, *Medicaid: Alternative Measures Could Be Used to Allocate Funding More Equitably*, GAO-13-434 (Washington, D.C.: May 10, 2013).

[107] See GAO, *High-Risk Series: An Update*. GAO-03-119 (Washington, D.C.: Jan. 1, 2003).

[108] See GAO-15-290.

[109] PPACA required the establishment of health insurance exchanges in each state by January 1, 2014, to allow consumers to compare individual health insurance options available in that state and enroll in coverage. In states electing not to operate their own state-based exchange, PPACA requires the federal government to establish and operate an exchange in the state, referred to as the federally facilitated exchange. State-based exchanges and federally facilitated exchanges are also referred to as marketplaces.

[110] Along with the "no wrong door" policy, CMS envisioned streamlined enrollment processes that include the real-time transfer of applications between state Medicaid agencies and the federally facilitated exchange, and immediate eligibility determinations. While a CMS official acknowledged that real time application transfers continued to be a goal, he did not anticipate this occurring until 2015 or 2016, given variability in states' abilities. See GAO-15-169.

[111] In March 2015, CBO projected that the number of individuals ever enrolled in Medicaid during the year would increase from 83 million in 2015 to 93 million in 2020. CBO, *Medicaid-Baseline Projections: March 2015 Baseline* (Washington, D.C.: March 9, 2015).

[112] While expenditures grew at an average annual rate of 5.3 percent between 2005 and 2015, the CMS Office of the Actuary has projected that the rate of increase will rise to 5.8 percent between 2015 and 2020. See CMS, *2014 Actuarial Report on the Financial Outlook for Medicaid*.

[113] See GAO-15-290.

[114] See GAO-15-239, GAO-14-689R, and GAO-13-384.

[115] The Iowa demonstration provides some—but not all—Medicaid required benefits that are not covered by private health insurance.

[116] See GAO-14-341.

[117] HHS OIG, *State Standards for Access to Care in Medicaid Managed Care*, OEI-02-11-00320 (Washington, D.C., September 2014); and *Access to Care: Provider Availability in Medicaid Managed Care*, OEI-02-13-00670 (Washington, D.C.: December 2014).

[118] Under section 1332 of PPACA, states will be able to apply for federal waivers of certain health insurance exchange requirements established under PPACA, and obtain from the federal government the amount of tax credits and cost-sharing reductions that would have been paid to state residents in the absence of a waiver. 42 U.S.C. § 18052.

[119] CBO, *Technological Change and the Growth of Health Care Spending* (Washington, D.C.: January 2008), 12.

[120] Federal law requires manufacturers to pay rebates to state Medicaid agencies for drugs dispensed to Medicaid enrollees. 42 U.S.C. § 1396r-8. See GAO, *Prescription Drugs: Comparison of DOD, Medicaid, and Medicare Part D Retail Reimbursement Prices,* GAO-14-578 (Washington, D.C.: June 30, 2014).

In: Key Issues Facing Medicaid
Editor: Jimmy Phillips

ISBN: 978-1-63484-647-9
© 2016 Nova Science Publishers, Inc.

Chapter 2

BACKGROUND MEMO FOR THE HEARING ON "MEDICAID AT 50: STRENGTHENING AND SUSTAINING THE PROGRAM"[*]

Staff of the House Committee on Energy and Commerce

TO: Members, Subcommittee on Health
FROM: Committee Majority Staff
RE: Hearing: "Medicaid at 50: Strengthening and Sustaining the Program."

I. INTRODUCTION

On Wednesday, July 8, at 10:15 a.m. in 2322 of the Rayburn House Office Building, the Subcommittee on Health will hold a hearing entitled, "Medicaid at 50: Strengthening and Sustaining the Program."

---

[*] This is an edited, reformatted and augmented version of a document prepared for a July 8, 2015 hearing of the House Committee on Energy and Commerce, Subcommittee on Health.

II. WITNESSES

- Vikki Wachino, Deputy Administrator, Centers for Medicare & Medicaid Services (CMS) and Director, Center for Medicaid and CHIP Services, CMS;
- Anne Schwartz, Executive Director, Medicaid and CHIP Payment and Access Commission (MACPAC).

III. BACKGROUND

Medicaid Overview

Created in 1965 as a joint federal-state program to finance health care coverage to serve low-income Americans and the indigent, Medicaid turns 50 years-old this year. Today, Medicaid is the world's largest health insurance program. Medicaid currently covers more than 71 million Americans—more than Medicare—and up to 83 million may be covered at any one point in a given year.[1] The Federal government currently spends more general tax revenue on Medicaid than it does on Medicare. During Fiscal Year 2016, the federal share of Medicaid outlays is expected to be approximately $344.4 billion.

Today, Medicaid accounts for more than 15 percent of all health care spending in the United States and plays an increasingly large role in our nation's health care system.[2] Representing roughly one in every four dollars in a state's average budget, Medicaid accounts for nearly half of national spending on long-term services and supports, and roughly a quarter of all mental health and substance abuse treatment spending. At the same time, Medicaid, along with the Children's Health Insurance Program (CHIP), pays for roughly half of all births in the United States each year.[3]

The federal government establishes specific parameters and minimum requirements for the program, while states administer their own Medicaid programs, thus effectively creating 56 different Medicaid programs—one for each state, territory, and the District of Columbia. Importantly, there are key waiver authorities that allow states, with CMS approval, to operate all or parts of their Medicaid program outside of statutory requirements:

- *Section 1115 Research & Demonstration Projects.* States may apply for program flexibility to test new or existing approaches to financing and delivering Medicaid and CHIP.
- *Section 1915(b) Managed Care Waivers.* States may apply for waivers to provide services through managed care delivery systems or otherwise limit people's choice of providers.
- *Section 1915(c) Home and Community-Based Services Waivers.* States may apply for waivers to provide long-term services and supports in home and community settings rather than institutional settings.

For purposes of brevity, given the complexity and scope of the program, some generalizations are necessary about Medicaid's eligible populations, benefits, and financing.

- *Eligibility.* Eligibility for Medicaid is determined by both federal and state law, whereby states set eligibility criteria within federal minimum standards. Individuals must meet both categorical eligibility and financial criteria. Some eligibility groups are mandatory, meaning that all states with a Medicaid program must cover them; others are optional. Medicaid statute also requires beneficiaries to meet federal and state requirements regarding residency, immigration status, and documentation of U.S. citizenship.
- *Benefits.* Federal law outlines minimum benefit packages for most populations in state Medicaid programs, as well as alternative benefit plans (ABP) and special benefits or special rules regarding certain benefits for targeted populations. Because of the breadth of the populations that Medicaid covers, Medicaid offers some benefits that are not typically covered by insurance plans—like nursing facility care, home and personal care, and early and periodic screening, diagnosis, and treatment [EPSDT] services.[4] Medicaid also covers the premiums and cost-sharing for roughly 9 million seniors who are enrolled in both Medicare and Medicaid. Additionally, states may receive federal dollars for additional, optional benefits and services which a state provides.
- *Financing.* Under the program, states claim federal matching funds for Medicaid expenditures from CMS, which oversees the program at the federal level. CMS matches state expenditures on medical assistance based on the federal medical assistance percentage

(FMAP), which is set by a statutory formula and can be no lower than 50 percent. The FMAP is generally calculated annually and varies by state according to each state's per capita income relative to the U.S. per capita income.[5] The formula provides higher FMAP rates, or federal reimbursement rates, to states with lower per capita incomes and lower FMAP rates to states with higher per capita incomes.

While the federal government provides general guidelines for states regarding allowable funding sources for the non-federal/state share of Medicaid expenditures, there is significant variation among states in the funding sources they use to finance their Medicaid program. States may use state general funds as well as provider taxes, local government funds, etc. to finance the state share of Medicaid (up 60 percent of state shares may come from local government funding).[6]

KEY CHANGES IN RECENT YEARS

The last two decades have seen marked changes in the footprint of the Medicaid program, with enrollment and expenditures increasingly rather dramatically since the early 1990s.[7] However, some of the most sweeping changes to the program have occurred in recent years.

Patient Protection and Affordable Care Act. PPACA made a number of modifications to Medicaid that, taken together, represent the most significant expansion and changes to the program since its creation in 1965.

Historically, Medicaid eligibility was largely limited to low-income children, pregnant women, parents of dependent children, elderly individuals, and individuals with disabilities. However, PPACA included a Medicaid expansion, which (subsequent to the Supreme Court's ruling in *NFIB vs. Sebelius*), allowed states to expand Medicaid eligibility to individuals under the age of 65 with income up to 133 percent of the federal poverty level (FPL) (effectively 138 percent FPL). PPACA also provided enhanced federal funding for coverage of this new expansion population, with the federal government covering 100 percent of the costs through 2016. The FMAP gradually diminishes to 90 percent by 2020.

In addition to the Medicaid expansion, as the Congressional Research Service summarized, PPACA:

Background Memo for the Hearing on "Medicaid at 50   91

- expanded eligibility for children ages 6 to 18 and former foster care children;
- transitioned to calculating income using a modified adjusted gross income (MAGI)
- methodology for most non-elderly beneficiaries;
- required ABP coverage for certain Medicaid beneficiaries;
- modified program integrity activities; and
- provided CMS with expansion demonstration authority for dual eligibles.

Managed Care. With the growing cost and complexity of the program, states have increasingly turned to managed care plans as a tool to help manage their Medicaid programs. Today, roughly three-fourths of all Medicaid beneficiaries are enrolled in some type of managed care plan.[8] As MACPAC explains, "compared with fee for service, managed care can allow for greater accountability for outcomes and can better support systematic efforts to measure, report, and monitor performance, access, and quality" and "may provide an opportunity for improved care management and care coordination."[9] CMS notes that an increasing number of states are using Managed Long Term Services and Supports (MLTSS) "as a strategy for expanding home- and community-based services, promoting community inclusion, ensuring quality and increasing efficiency."[10]

On May 26, 2015, CMS published the Medicaid and CHIP Managed Care Notice of Proposed Rulemaking (CMS 2390-P), which proposes to modernize Medicaid and CHIP managed care regulations.[11] This proposed rule is the first major update to Medicaid and CHIP managed care regulations in more than a decade.

Home and Community-Based Services. With LTSS accounting for over a quarter of Medicaid expenditures and expected to increase in coming years with the aging of the baby boom population, states are increasingly turning to home and community-based services (HCBS) to provide care. Last year, CMS finalized a rule related to several sections of Medicaid law under which states may use federal Medicaid funds to pay for HCBS.

EVOLVING CHALLENGES FACING THE PROGRAM

As Medicaid turns 50 this year, the program faces a rapidly evolving policy landscape— which presents both challenges and opportunities. For Medicaid to be strengthened and sustained as a vital safety net to provide needed care for our nation's most vulnerable patients for coming decades, Congress and CMS will undoubtedly be forced to make changes to the program in the years ahead. As GAO has noted, "the effects of unprecedented changes recently made to the Medicaid program will continue to emerge in the coming years and are likely to exacerbate the challenges and shortcomings that already exist in federal oversight and management of the program."[12] There are a number of challenges which may merit Congressional or administrative review and action.

Long-Term Services and Supports. The Medicaid program allows for the coverage of LTSS through several possible state delivery models and over a continuum of settings, including institutional care and HCBS. This part of the Medicaid program has seen renewed focus in recent years, with the termination of the CLASS Act (created in PPACA) and Congress's creation of the Commission on Long-Term Care.[13] With the aging of the Baby Boomers, LTSS will continue to represent an important benefit for millions of Americans—as well as being a significant driver of overall spending growth.

Federal Financial Sustainability. According to CBO, the Federal share of Medicaid outlays are expected roughly to double over the coming decade, increasing from $270 billion in 2014, to more than $529 billion in 2024.[14] Medicaid spending already consumes roughly one in four State dollars. Based on current trends, by 2025, *each year* Medicaid will cost Federal and State taxpayers more than $1 trillion and will cover more than 98 million Americans at some point that year.[15] CBO has warned repeatedly that the continued growth of our entitlements, including Medicaid, is the single largest structural driver of our debt and deficits. Specifically, CBO warned that "[t]he long-term outlook for the federal budget has worsened dramatically over the past several years, in the wake of the 2007–2009 recession and slow recovery."[16] Unless Congress changes course, according to CBO data, by 2030 the entire federal budget will be spent on debt payments, Social Security, and our health care entitlements.[17]

State Financing. Because states finance *no more than half* of the total cost of their Medicaid programs, states may have mixed incentives with regard to overseeing the financial growth of the program. This dynamic is particularly exacerbated due to a number of funding sources states have used, including some financing mechanisms designed to maximize the amount of federal Medicaid funds coming to the state. For example, in 2014, GAO found that "states financed 26 percent, or over $46 billion, of the nonfederal share of Medicaid expenditures with funds from health care providers and local governments in state fiscal year 2012."[18] Although such financing arrangements are allowed under certain conditions, GAO noted such arrangements "can also result in shifting costs to the federal government with limited benefits to providers and beneficiaries." The Inspector General's Office at HHS noted a similar concern, saying, such state policies distort the federal-state partnership, "causing the Federal Government to pay more than its share of Medicaid expenditures," while not yielding "any increase in benefit to beneficiaries... at the expense of the Federal Government and, ultimately, Federal taxpayers."[19] The President's *National Commission on Fiscal Responsibility and Reform* recommended that Congress reduce and eventually phase out state's ability to use provider taxes to fund Medicaid.[20] Other state financing schemes include intergovernmental transfers and payment policies like DSH or other supplemental payments that effectively draw down federal funds without expending a proportional amount of state general funds.

Medicaid Expansion. Adding to the significant uptick in annual Medicaid outlays is the categorical expansion of Medicaid to childless adults under PPACA. CBO has estimated the Medicaid and CHIP coverage provisions under PPACA will cost taxpayers roughly $800 billion over the 2015-2024 period.[21] PPACA included "newly eligible" FMAP rates for childless adults that were notably higher than any other FMAP. Under the "newly eligible" FMAP rate, from 2014 through 2016, states receive a 100% FMAP rate for the cost of individuals who are "newly eligible" for Medicaid due to the ACA expansion. This "newly eligible" FMAP rate phases down to 95 percent in 2017 and following years so that by 2020 it is 90 percent where it remains thereafter under current law. While the enhanced FMAP for this population may cost less per enrollee than traditional Medicaid populations, some have raised questions regarding the appropriateness of the federal government covering a higher percentage of the cost of care for adults above poverty compared to disabled, elderly, or children below poverty. Additionally, the states who have expanded coverage under PPACA through a five-year 1115 demonstration waiver may face administrative or financial hurdles in renewing those waivers in their current form.

Program Vulnerabilities. The Medicaid program was designated by GAO as a high risk program more than a decade ago due to "its size, growth, diversity of programs, and concerns about the adequacy of fiscal oversight."

While the shared federal-state nature of the program leads to significant variability, nationally, Medicaid is a program facing significant program integrity challenges. The federal error rate for Medicaid payments is high – and was recently adjusted upwards.[22] Additionally, due to a number of factors, many state Medicaid programs suffer from significant waste, fraud, and abuse, due to failures in state and federal oversight and enforcement actions. For example, a recent GAO report found thousands of beneficiaries had payments made on their behalf concurrently by two or more state Medicaid programs, while hundreds of deceased beneficiaries received millions of dollars in Medicaid benefits subsequent to the beneficiary's death.[23] Unfortunately, such lapses can also negatively impact patient safety. GAO found dozens of providers who were excluded from federal health-care programs, including Medicaid, for a variety of reasons that include patient abuse or neglect, fraud, theft, bribery, or tax evasion were still being paid by the program. The Inspector General's office at HHS has found repeated cases of fraud, abuse, or neglect in Medicaid personal care services – services owed to some of the nation's most vulnerable patients.[24]

Quality and Access to Care. Timely access to the right care provided by the right provider in the right setting is often a concern because of the needs and vulnerability of the individuals covered by Medicaid, including children, the elderly, and the disabled. Nationally, only a portion of primary health care providers accept Medicaid beneficiaries—often with even fewer specialists accepting such patients.[25] GAO noted that while national survey data have suggested that access reported by Medicaid beneficiaries is adequate, results for individual beneficiaries may vary greatly by location, provider relationships, and a number of other factors. Moreover, GAO has found that Medicaid beneficiaries do face particular challenges in accessing certain types of care.[26] Some research has suggested that, at least in some studies, Medicaid beneficiaries have not experienced notably better health outcomes than individuals with no health coverage – raising additional questions about the quality and timeliness of access for Medicaid patients.[27] Given the growing role of Medicaid in our health system, it will be critical in the future to continue to evaluate the quality of care and access to care that vulnerable Medicaid patients receive.

Growth of 1115 Waivers. Section 1115 of the Social Security Act (Act) authorizes the Secretary of HHS to waive certain federal Medicaid requirements and allow costs that would not otherwise be eligible for federal matching funds for experimental, pilot or demonstration projects that, in the Secretary's judgment, are likely to assist in promoting Medicaid objectives.[28]

Background Memo for the Hearing on "Medicaid at 50   95

In recent years, 1115 demonstrations have been used by some states to expand Medicaid under PPACA.[29] Section 1115 demonstrations also have been used by six states to implement Delivery System Reform Incentive Payment (DSRIP) programs, which provide Medicaid funds for states to make supplemental payments that would not otherwise be permitted under federal managed care rules and as tools for investing in provider-led efforts intended to improve health care quality and access.[30] Section 1115 demonstrations account for a significant and growing proportion of federal Medicaid expenditures. GAO has noted that in fiscal year 2014, section 1115 demonstrations accounted for close to *one-third* of total Medicaid expenditures.[31] Yet, GAO found that in fiscal year 2011, "$57.5 billion in federal funds, or about one-fifth of the $260 billion in federal Medicaid expenditures, were for services, coverage initiatives, and delivery system redesigns provided under section 1115 demonstrations in 40 states."[32] Recent Congressional oversight has raised serious concerns over the Administration's process for approving 1115 demonstrations, including the approval criteria used, the timeframe for review, adherence to budget neutrality concerns, and other issues.[33]

End Notes

[1] http://www.medicaid.gov/medicaid-chip-program-information/program-information/ down loads/april-2015-enrollment-report.pdf and http://www.cbo.gov/sites/default/files/cbofiles/ attachments/44204-2015-03-Medicaid.pdf.

[2] https://www.macpac.gov/wp-content/uploads/2015/01/Table-16.-National-Health-Expenditures -by-Type-andPayer-2012.pdf.

[3] http://www.crs.gov/pdfloader/R43357.

[4] http://www.crs.gov/pdfloader/R43357.

[5] States' FMAPs: https://www.macpac.gov/wp-content/uploads/2015/01/Federal-Medical-Assistance-PercentagesFMAPs-and-Enhanced-FMAPs-E-FMAPs-by-State-FY-2012–FY-2016.pdf.

[6] http://www.crs.gov/pdfloader/R43357.

[7] https://www.macpac.gov/wp-content/uploads/2015/01/Figure-1.-Medicaid-Enrollment-and-Spending-FY-1966-FY-2013.pdf.

[8] http://medicaid.gov/medicaid-chip-program-information/by-topics/data-and-systems/down loads/2011-medicaidmc-enrollment-report.pdf.

[9] https://www.macpac.gov/subtopic/managed-care/.

[10] http://www.medicaid.gov/Medicaid-CHIP-Program-Information/By-Topics/Delivery-Sys tems/MedicaidManaged-Long-Term-Services-and-Supports-MLTSS.html.

[11] https://www.federalregister.gov/articles/2015/06/01/2015-12965/medicaid-and-childrens-health-insuranceprogram-chip-programs-medicaid-managed-care-chip-delivered.

[12] http://www.gao.gov/highrisk/medicaid_program/why_did_study#t=1.

96   Staff of the House Committee on Energy and Commerce

[13] http://ltccommission.org/.

[14] http://www.cbo.gov/sites/default/files/cbofiles/attachments/44204-2015-03-Medicaid.pdf.

[15] Spending estimates based on projections of National Health Expenditure data from CMS, http://www.cms.gov/Research-Statistics-Data-and-Systems/Statistics-Trends-and-Reports/NationalHealthExpendData/NationalHealthAccountsProjected.html. Medicaid spending for 2024 and 2025 was further estimated assuming an annual rate of growth of 6.5 percent. Enrollment projection from CBO's Medicaid baseline, https://www.cbo.gov/sites/default/files/cbofiles/attachments/44204-2014-04-Medicaid.pdf.

[16] http://www.cbo.gov/publication/50250.

[17] Check stat with Budget tables.

[18] http://www.gao.gov/products/GAO-14-627.

[19] http://oig.hhs.gov/newsroom/spotlight/2014/inflated-federal-costs.asp.

[20] https://www.fiscalcommission.gov/sites/fiscalcommission.gov/files/documents/TheMomentofTruth12_1_2010.pdf, page 39.

[21] http://www.cbo.gov/sites/default/files/45231-ACA_Estimates.pdf.

[22] https://paymentaccuracy.gov/tracked/medicaid-2014#learnmore and http://energycommerce.house.gov/ pressrelease/committee-leaders-question-administration%E2%80%99s-decision-ease-fraud-reduction-targets.

[23] http://www.gao.gov/assets/680/670208.pdf.

[24] https://oig.hhs.gov/reports-and-publications/portfolio/portfolio-12-12-01.pdf.

[25] https://www.macpac.gov/wp-content/uploads/2015/01/Table-23.-Provider-Availability-Measures-of-Access-toCare-for-Medicaid-CHIP-Beneficiaries-2012.pdf.

[26] http://www.gao.gov/highrisk/medicaid_program/why_did_study#t=1.

[27] http://www.nejm.org/doi/full/10.1056/NEJMp1108222.

[28] http://www.ssa.gov/OP_Home/ssact/title11/1115.htm. Note: While the statute gives this authority to the Secretary of HHS, most of the oversight of Medicaid demonstrations is delegated to the Administrator of the Centers for Medicare and Medicaid Services (CMS).

[29] http://files.kff.org/attachment/issue-brief-the-aca-and-medicaid-expansion-waivers.

[30] In its June 2015 report, MACPAC indicated that clear and consistent federal guidance about DSRIP program design, policies, and goals is needed.

[31] http://www.gao.gov/assets/670/669582.pdf.

[32] GAO report GAO-13-384, page 2.

[33] http://energycommerce.house.gov/press-release/subhealth-continues-efforts-protect-most-vulnerable.

In: Key Issues Facing Medicaid
Editor: Jimmy Phillips

ISBN: 978-1-63484-647-9
© 2016 Nova Science Publishers, Inc.

Chapter 3

STATEMENT OF VIKKI WACHINO, DEPUTY ADMINISTRATOR AND DIRECTOR, CENTER FOR MEDICAID AND CHIP SERVICES, CENTERS FOR MEDICARE AND MEDICAID SERVICES. HEARING ON "MEDICAID AT 50: STRENGTHENING AND SUSTAINING THE PROGRAM"[*]

Chairman Pitts, Ranking Member Green, and members of the Subcommittee, thank you for the invitation and the opportunity to discuss the importance of the Medicaid program, reflect on some of its achievements over the past 50 years, and discuss the Centers for Medicare & Medicaid Services' (CMS') work with states in key areas such as broadening access to coverage, strengthening the quality of care through payment and delivery system reforms, and enhancing the program so that it meets the needs of our beneficiaries most effectively.

The Medicaid program provides health insurance coverage for more than 70 million Americans, playing a particularly important role in providing coverage for low-income children, adults, pregnant women, people with disabilities, and seniors. The health insurance coverage Medicaid provides ranges from prenatal and pediatric care, to preventive care aimed at stemming

---

[*] This is an edited, reformatted and augmented version of a statement presented July 8, 2015 before the House Committee on Energy and Commerce, Subcommittee on Health.

chronic diseases, to long term care services and supports. Federal financial support and flexibilities in program rules, along with new tools and options made available through the Affordable Care Act, have helped provide a platform for CMS and states to adopt a range of improvements and innovations in their Medicaid programs. Under the Affordable Care Act, Medicaid eligibility has been simplified and aligned across coverage programs. Thanks to these simplifications and the availability of Medicaid coverage to more low-income adults, millions more uninsured Americans are gaining coverage.

Because Medicaid is jointly funded by states and the Federal Government and is administered by states within Federal guidelines, both the Federal Government and states have key roles as stewards of the program, and CMS and states work together closely to carry out these responsibilities. Under the Medicaid Federal-state partnership, the Federal Government sets forth a policy framework for the program and states have significant flexibility to choose options that enable them to deliver high quality, cost-efficient care for their residents. CMS is committed to working with states and other partners to advance efforts that promote health, improve the quality of care, and lower health care costs.

This month we mark the 50th anniversary of the Medicaid program. For five decades, Medicaid has helped facilitate access to needed health services and provided financial security through protection from high out-of-pocket costs for millions of low-income Americans. Medicaid has played a vital role in providing comprehensive care for children that helps support their growth, school readiness, and development into healthy adults. Medicaid has also supported working families whose employers do not offer affordable health insurance, and fostered better health for pregnant women and positive birth outcomes for their babies by facilitating access to critical prenatal services. It has helped address the frequently complex health needs of people with disabilities, and supported them in living independently. And it has covered long-term care services and supports for millions of America's seniors and works in concert with Medicare to meet critical health needs. Over time, Medicaid has also risen to new challenges, providing care for people with HIV and AIDS, meeting the screening and treatment needs of people with breast and cervical cancer, and contributing to financial stability for low-income families by helping them maintain coverage during economic downturns.

Medicaid plays a fundamental role in assuring that low-income people have access to a high level of care. According to survey research released by the Commonwealth Fund last month, 95 percent of adults who had continuous Medicaid coverage in 2014 had a regular source of care, and the percentage of people who rated the quality of the care they received in the past 12 months as excellent or very good was comparable to that of people enrolled in private coverage. Adults enrolled in Medicaid also reported getting key preventive services like blood pressure checks at higher rates than did individuals who were uninsured. And Medicaid beneficiaries were less likely to have had problems paying medical bills than did individuals who had private coverage or who were uninsured. They were also less likely than those who were uninsured to skip getting medical care or to let a prescription go unfilled due to cost.[1]

Recent research that examined the long-term impact of Medicaid on the population it serves demonstrates that it is a sound investment for the Nation. Earlier this year, researchers at the National Bureau of Economic Research reported the results of longitudinal research that examined children enrolled in Medicaid and the Children's Health Insurance Program (CHIP) over time. They found that being enrolled in Medicaid and CHIP confers substantial benefits on individuals, and the country as a whole, when they reach adulthood. Specifically, the researchers found that individuals who were eligible for Medicaid and CHIP as children had higher cumulative wages as adults than their peers. The researchers estimated that the Federal Government recoups 56 cents of each dollar spent on childhood Medicaid by the time those children reach age 60.[2]

As we approach Medicaid's 50th anniversary, CMS is building on Medicaid's past successes and enhancing the program. Today I would like to highlight some of the key areas in which CMS is working with states to strengthen the program's ability to serve its beneficiaries:

- modernizing the eligibility and enrollment process for Medicaid and CHIP to support a strong consumer experience;
- expanding Medicaid eligibility to decrease the number of uninsured Americans and lower the costs of uncompensated care;
- strengthening payment and delivery systems reform to encourage coordinated, high quality, patient-centered care;
- continuing to advance the ability of seniors and people with disabilities to receive home and community-based care;
- updating the Medicaid managed care rules to promote quality, transparency, and access to care and to align with the rules of other payers;

- enhancing data systems to more accurately measure health care quality and strengthen program integrity and Medicaid financial management; and
- strengthening program integrity efforts to better combat and prevent fraud, waste, and abuse.

MODERNIZING MEDICAID AND CHIP ELIGIBILITY AND ENROLLMENT PROCESSES

In our implementation of the Affordable Care Act, CMS has substantially simplified and modernized Medicaid and CHIP rules and processes for most people who apply for Medicaid and CHIP, creating an enrollment process that helps eligible consumers enroll in Medicaid and CHIP and access their coverage more quickly and smoothly. These rules are designed to align and coordinate with policies and procedures established for people who enroll in qualified health plans through the Marketplace. Before these changes, consumers would often encounter a paper-dependent process that was unnecessarily complex and time intensive, sometimes involving long waits for a decision on a family's eligibility that posed logistical challenges for working families and could delay access to needed care.

Now, consumers can use a single, streamlined application to apply for Medicaid, CHIP, and qualified health plans through the Marketplace. Consumers can apply online, over the phone, or by mail, and can get help from application assistors in their communities, or via call centers that help people apply for coverage. CMS and states have established an electronic approach to verifying financial and non-financial information needed to determine Medicaid, CHIP, and Marketplace eligibility. States now rely on available electronic data sources to confirm data included on the application, facilitating faster eligibility decisions and promoting program integrity. In addition, simplified renewal processes help ensure that people retain Medicaid and CHIP coverage for as long as they are eligible, and that beneficiaries who remain eligible get needed services like prescription medications.

Modernized state eligibility and enrollment systems underpin many of these simplifications by enabling automated eligibility verification, offering online applications and streamlining the consumer experience. To help states invest in these systems, CMS made available 90-percent matching funds through December 31, 2015, for eligibility system design and development, and the enhanced 75-percent matching rate indefinitely for maintenance and operations of such systems provided that these systems met certain standards and conditions that were designed to support a simple, streamlined enrollment process. In April, in a Notice of Proposed Rulemaking, CMS proposed ongoing access to the 90-percent and 75-percent matching authority for eligibility and enrollment systems to provide states with additional time to complete their full systems modernization, retire outdated "legacy" systems, and promote a dynamic, integrated, enterprise approach to Medicaid information technology systems. Refinements were made to the standards and conditions to ensure optimal systems development and efficient use of state and Federal funding.

As a result of these simplifications and systems improvements, states are making substantial progress processing Medicaid and CHIP applications more efficiently, often in real or near real-time. For example, in Washington, 92 percent of applications are processed in under 24 hours; in New York, 80 percent of applications are processed in one session; and in Rhode Island, 66 percent of applications are processed without manual intervention or the requirement of additional information.

EXPANDING MEDICAID ELIGIBILITY

As a result of the Affordable Care Act, states have the opportunity to expand Medicaid eligibility to individuals ages 19-64 years of age with incomes up to 133 percent of the Federal poverty level (FPL). For the first time, states can provide Medicaid coverage for low-income adults without dependent children without the need for a demonstration waiver. The Affordable Care Act provides full Federal funding to cover newly eligible adults in states that expand Medicaid up to 133 percent FPL through Calendar Year 2016, and covers no less than 90 percent of costs thereafter. This increased Federal support has enabled 28 states and the District of Columbia to expand Medicaid coverage to more low-income adults. Most recently, in January, Indiana expanded its efforts to bring much needed access to health care coverage to uninsured low-income residents. Primarily as a result of the expansion of coverage to low-income adults and the eligibility and enrollment simplifications CMS and states have made, 12.3 million people have gained Medicaid or CHIP coverage since the beginning of the Affordable Care Act's first open enrollment period.[3]

States that have expanded their Medicaid programs are documenting significant reductions in uncompensated care and the uninsured rate. Hospitals provided over $50 billion in uncompensated care in 2013; in 2014, there was a $7.4 billion reduction in uncompensated care costs, and with 68 percent of the reduction coming from states expanding Medicaid.[4] And of the 11 states with the greatest reductions in uninsured rates in 2015, 10 had expanded Medicaid eligibility.[5] This coverage is translating into tangible improvements in population health. Nearly one-third of the cases of diabetes in the United States have not been diagnosed; however, in states that expanded Medicaid, the number of beneficiaries with newly identified diabetes rose by 23 percent, compared to 0.4 percent in states that did not expand Medicaid, in the first six months of 2014.[6]

CMS is committed to working with states to expand Medicaid in ways that work for them, while protecting the integrity of the program and those it serves. For example, in Iowa and Arkansas, under section 1115(a) demonstrations, some new Medicaid enrollees receive their coverage from Qualified Health Plans offered in the individual market through the Marketplace. Michigan's Health and Wellness Plan promotes healthy behaviors through education and engagement of beneficiaries and providers. Iowa's demonstration includes a Healthy Behaviors program under which a beneficiary is eligible to reduce his/her premium payment amount by engaging in health improvement activities.

ACCELERATING STATES' EFFORTS ON MEDICAID DELIVERY SYSTEM REFORM

States and CMS share a strong interest in achieving better health and better care at lower cost. Medicaid plays a major role in the health care delivery system, and funds 16 percent of the Nation's health care services.[7] The expansion of Medicaid to new populations presents both states and CMS with additional opportunities to pursue delivery system reforms that improve the Medicaid patient experience while helping to drive innovation across the health care system. CMS is engaged in a variety of initiatives to work with states, providers, and other stakeholders to help spur innovation. CMS has collaborated with states in key areas to improve the quality of care and reform payment and delivery systems, has worked with innovator states to advance specific reforms, has provided states with tools and guidance developed to meet the needs of Medicaid beneficiaries, and is working to measure and improve quality across states, in coordination with similar efforts underway in Medicare and in the private market.

Earlier this year, Department of Health and Human Services (HHS) Secretary Burwell announced measurable goals and a timeline to move the Medicare program, and the health care system at large, toward paying providers based on the quality, rather than the quantity of care they provide. This initiative will ultimately create a payment environment that appropriately promotes and rewards better care management for persons with chronic illness. CMS is dedicated to working with states to advance delivery system reforms that support these goals throughout the Medicaid and CHIP programs.

Strong Start

The Strong Start for Mothers and Newborns initiative includes two strategies to reduce premature births: first, working with hospitals to reduce the number of early elective deliveries across all payers; and second, testing models of enhanced prenatal care to reduce preterm births among women covered by Medicaid or CHIP.

The first strategy is a public-private partnership and awareness campaign to reduce the rate of non-medically indicated early elective deliveries prior to 39 weeks. Working together with Partnership for Patients, HHS sponsored public-private efforts to improve the safety, reliability, and cost of hospital care. The Partnership for Patients is an initiative that works with providers to identify potential hospital safety solutions and test models for improving care transitions from the hospital to other settings, and for reducing readmissions for high-risk Medicare beneficiaries. CMS collaborated with Hospital Engagement Networks, a group of providers that work at the regional, state, national, or hospital system level to help identify solutions already working and disseminate them to other hospitals and providers, across the country to identify and spread best practices to reduce potentially unnecessary early elective deliveries, which contributed to a 70.4-percent reduction in early elective deliveries between 2010 and 2013 among participating hospitals. For example, the Ohio Perinatal Quality Collaborative used a range of interventions to shift almost 21,000 births from between 36-38 weeks' gestation to 39 weeks gestation between September 2008 and October 2011. This shift reduced NICU admissions by three percent (approximately 621 admissions), which alone resulted in an estimated $24.8 million in savings for the three year period. Almost half of these births were to mothers enrolled in Medicaid.

The second Strong Start strategy is a four-year initiative to test new approaches to prenatal care and evaluate enhanced prenatal care interventions for women enrolled in Medicaid or CHIP who are at risk for having a preterm birth. The goal of the initiative is to determine if these approaches to care can reduce the rate of preterm births, improve the health outcomes of pregnant women and newborns, and decrease the anticipated total cost of medical care during pregnancy, delivery and over the first year of life. The initiative is currently supporting service delivery through 27 awardees and 213 provider sites, across 30 states, the District of Columbia, and Puerto Rico. While more thorough analysis must be completed, preliminary findings after year one of the program suggest that the enhanced prenatal care models may have a positive effect on some birth outcomes — specifically, increased rates of breastfeeding, decreased rates of cesarean section delivery, and decreased rates of preterm birth in comparison to national averages.

Health Homes

The Affordable Care Act created an optional Medicaid State Plan benefit that allows states to establish Health Homes in order to better coordinate care for people with Medicaid who have chronic conditions. Health Home providers operate under a "whole person" philosophy to integrate and coordinate all primary, acute, and behavioral health care, and long-term care services and supports, and to measure quality of care. Through this program, states receive a 90-percent enhanced Federal Medical Assistance Percentage (FMAP) for health home services for the first eight quarters and receive their regular match rate thereafter.

To date, CMS has approved Health Home State Plan Amendments in 19 states, the first of which was Missouri. Missouri's Medicaid program, in conjunction with its Department of Mental Health, successfully launched two Health Home initiatives: one designed to improve care for Medicaid beneficiaries with physical health conditions and one for beneficiaries with behavioral health conditions. Under these initiatives, participating Health Home providers delivered patient-centered culturally sensitive care, enhanced care management and care coordination across health care settings, and improved access to individual and family supports, including referral to community, social support, and recovery services. Missouri's Health Home programs reported reductions in-hospital admissions per 1000 of 12.8 percent and 5.9 percent, respectively, while emergency-room usage per 1000 also declined by 8.2 percent and 9.7 percent in each program. The state is also reporting an improvement in several key clinical indicators, including hemoglobin A1C levels in participants with diabetes mellitus, as well as LDL cholesterol levels and systolic and diastolic blood pressures in participants with heart disease.

Innovative State Delivery System Models

Many State Medicaid agencies have started using a variety of approaches to improve and modernize their delivery and payment systems. For example, in 2012, Oregon launched a new managed care model, creating Coordinated Care Organizations (CCOs) that are risk-bearing, locally-governed provider networks that deliver community-driven coordinated care to Medicaid beneficiaries. These entities provide all Medicaid enrollees with physical, behavioral, and dental health services. The CCOs are paid via a global Medicaid budget that grows at a fixed rate, while allowing for some flexibility in the services that a plan provides. Oregon is held to quality and spending metrics to ensure that quality continues to improve as the state and CCOs control costs. The CCOs are held accountable for performance-based metrics and quality standards that align with industry standards, new systems of governance, and payment incentives that reward improved health outcomes. CMS has also worked with states to advance integrated care models like patient centered medical homes and accountable care organizations.

Delivery System Reform Incentive Program

CMS works with interested states to pursue state-initiated and developed delivery system reform initiatives. Through Delivery System Reform Incentive Payment (DSRIP) programs, authorized through section 1115(a) demonstrations, states support hospitals and other providers in enhancing how they provide Medicaid services. The first DSRIP initiatives were approved in 2010, and the most recent initiative will begin this year. The lessons learned over this period of time have helped CMS to refine the DSRIP initiatives and focus them on sustainable, beneficiary-focused changes to how providers are organized and how care is paid for under the Medicaid program. Currently, eight states have section 1115(a) demonstrations with DSRIP programs.

These initiatives are continuing to evolve, with the most recently approved DSRIP program providing funding for a broader set of providers, more specific evaluation metrics, and requirements to meet statewide goals. CMS will continue to work with these states to design and evaluate both short- and long-term outcomes of these initiatives and the impacts they are having on care delivery, the costs of services, and the overall health of Medicaid beneficiaries.

Medicaid Innovation Accelerator Program

To spur innovation between CMS and the states, CMS created the Medicaid Innovation Accelerator Program (IAP) with the goal of improving health and health care for Medicaid beneficiaries by supporting states' ongoing payment and service delivery-reform efforts. The IAP is consistent with recommendations made by the National Governors Association Health Care Sustainability Task Force, which focused on system transformation and state innovations that rely on the redesign of health care delivery and payment systems. Through the IAP, states can receive targeted program support designed around their ongoing delivery and payment system-innovation efforts.

CMS selected four areas as IAP's program priorities in consultation with states and stakeholders: (1) substance use disorders; (2) Medicaid beneficiaries with high needs and high costs; (3) community integration to support long-term services and supports; and (4) physical and mental health integration. CMS has been working intensively with seven states over the past five months on the first priority area to develop and implement substance use disorder service delivery reform activities. Additionally, CMS announced the details of the second IAP program priority area, improving care for Medicaid beneficiaries with complex needs and high costs, at the end of June 2015 via a national webinar. The final two program priority areas, community integration to support long- term services and supports and physical and mental health integration, have target launch timeframes of fall and winter of 2015, respectively. CMS also is working with some states to support data integration across Medicare and Medicaid to provide integrated care for Medicare-Medicaid enrollees.

All states can be laboratories for health care reform. As noted above, 19 states have initiated comprehensive health homes for people with multiple chronic conditions. Several states have developed shared savings payment models through State Innovation Models. Twelve states are testing new delivery and payment models for people who are dually eligible for Medicaid and Medicare through the Financial Alignment Initiative. While payment and service delivery innovation is well underway in states, there are common challenges to all Medicaid delivery reforms, particularly in technical areas such as data analytics, payment modeling and financial simulations, quality measurement, and rapid cycle learning. IAP will help strengthen all of our efforts on delivery reform and move Medicaid payment and delivery to the next level by addressing these shared issues.

State Innovation Models

The CMS Innovation Center created the State Innovation Models (SIM) initiative for states that are prepared for or committed to planning, designing, testing, and supporting evaluation of new payment and service delivery models in the context of larger health system transformation. The SIM is providing financial and technical support to states for the development and testing of state-led, multi-payer health care payment and service delivery models that will improve health system performance, increase quality of care, and decrease costs for Medicare, Medicaid and CHIP beneficiaries.

In Round One of the SIM Initiative, 25 states were awarded funds to design or test innovative health care payment and service delivery models in the form of Model Design, Model Pre-Test, and Model Test awards. In Round Two,[8] the SIM Initiative is providing funds to 28 states, three territories, and the District of Columbia. This includes both Model Design awardees, states that are designing plans and strategies for statewide innovation, and Model Test awardees, states that are testing and implementing comprehensive statewide health transformation plans. Including the Round Two awardees, over half of states, representing 61 percent of the U.S. population, will be working to support comprehensive state-based innovation in health system transformation. Many of the states participating in SIM are developing new approaches to delivering care to Medicaid and CHIP beneficiaries. For example, in Maine, the SIM grant from CMS has supported the state to design a vision for a robust multi-payer model, including components such as health homes and shared savings.

Financial Alignment Initiative

Today there are over 10 million Americans enrolled in both the Medicare and Medicaid programs, commonly known as "dual eligible" beneficiaries. The Medicare-Medicaid Financial Alignment Initiative is designed to better align the financial incentives of the two programs to provide these dual eligible beneficiaries with improved health outcomes and a better care experience.

The Financial Alignment Initiative created two model types: capitated and managed fee-forservice. In the capitated model, a state, CMS, and a health plan enter into a three-way contract, and the plan receives a prospective blended payment to provide comprehensive, coordinated care. In the managed fee-for-service model, a state and CMS enter into an agreement by which the state is eligible to benefit from a portion of savings from initiatives designed to improve quality and reduce costs for both Medicare and Medicaid. Implementation of each demonstration is a collaborative effort between CMS and the state, and CMS has made several resources available to assist states with implementation activities. To date, new demonstrations are underway in 12 states, with approximately 400,000 dually-eligible beneficiaries participating in the financial-alignment models.

MOVING TOWARDS HOME AND COMMUNITY-BASED CARE

CMS continues to look for ways to enable Medicaid beneficiaries with disabilities to receive home and community-based care, instead of relying on institutional care. The commitment to deliver care in ways that improve both efficiency and beneficiary outcomes extends beyond the delivery of acute and outpatient care to the delivery of long term care services as well. The passage of the Affordable Care Act provides new and expanded opportunities to serve more individuals in home and community-based settings.

The core mechanism that states have used to promote access to community-based services and supports for Medicaid beneficiaries is through Home and Community-Based Services (HCBS) waivers. Today, 47 states and Washington, D.C. operate at least one 1915(c) HCBS waiver. The Affordable Care Act also created new options under state plan authority for states to provide home and community-based care. For example, the Affordable Care

Act authorized Community First Choice under section 1915(k), a state plan benefit that offers community-based attendant supports and services to individuals who meet institutional levels of care. Five states have approved Community First Choice state plan amendments and CMS is also working intensively with several additional states on proposals that are under review.

As states continue to reduce their reliance on institutional care, develop community-based longterm care opportunities, and transition individuals living in institutions to community living, almost all of them have worked with CMS as part of our Money Follows the Person Rebalancing Demonstration Grant Program. Today, 43 states and Washington, D.C. participate in Money Follows the Person and receive enhanced Federal matching funds to serve individuals who move from institutional care to community integrated long-term care settings. In addition to Money Follows the Person, 18 states currently participate in the Balancing Incentive Program, also created by the Affordable Care Act, which provides enhanced Federal match to states that make structural reforms to increase institutional diversion and access to non-institutional long-term care services. According to the forthcoming Long-Term Services and Supports (LTSS) Expenditure Report to be released by CMS, 2013 data show that Medicaid spending on such services has tipped in favor of the community, with51 percent spent on community-based services versus 49 percent being spent on institutional services. Ten years ago, community-based spending made up just 33 percent of total long-term care spending.

Medicaid has also helped ensure that individuals are the focal point of the HCBS care planning process and that they have choice of and control over HCBS services. HCBS programs have a person-centered planning requirement – a process directed by the individual with long-term care service and support needs which may include a representative chosen by the individual, and/or who is authorized to make personal or health decisions for the person, family members, legal guardians, friends, caregivers, and others the person or his/her representative wishes to include. HCBS programs also include the ability for an individual to "self-direct" their services. Participant or self-directed service options in long-term care financing programs provide individuals and their representatives the opportunity to hire, manage, and fire their direct-service workers. Funds may also be used to purchase other goods and services, such as assistive technology, home modifications, personal care supplies, and transportation, within Federal and state guidelines. At least 38 states have self-direction programs in place for HCBS and about one quarter of all Medicaid beneficiaries receiving HCBS are self-directing some of their services, according to state-reported data in 2014.

As we move to more home and community-based services, acknowledging that the majority of Medicaid spending is in the area of long-term care services and supports, CMS is engaged in making sure that the delivery of these services is supported by robust data. As such, we are engaged in testing an experience of care survey and a set of functional assessment elements, demonstrating the use of personal health records and creating a standard electronic long-term services and support plan. This work will provide national metrics and valuable feedback on how health information technology can be implemented in this component of the Medicaid program.

UPDATING MANAGED CARE

As the health care delivery system moves towards more integrated care and away from fee-forservice, states are increasingly moving to the use of managed care in serving Medicaid beneficiaries. Approximately 58 percent of Medicaid beneficiaries are enrolled in capitated, risk-based managed care for part or all of their services. Managed care is serving new populations, including seniors and people with disabilities who need long-term services and supports, and individuals newly eligible for Medicaid. Recognizing these changes, in May CMS issued a proposed rule to modernize Medicaid and CHIP managed care regulations to update the programs' rules and strengthen the delivery of quality care for beneficiaries. This proposed rule is the first major update to Medicaid and CHIP managed care regulations in more than a decade and a major part of CMS' efforts to strengthen delivery systems that serve Medicaid and CHIP beneficiaries.

The proposed rule incorporates several core principles to update the regulations, specifically aligning with Medicare Advantage and private coverage plans, supporting state delivery system reform, promoting the quality of care, strengthening program and fiscal integrity, incorporating best practices for managed long-term services and supports programs, and enhancing the beneficiary experience. Under the proposed rule, Medicaid managed care policies would be aligned to a much greater extent with those of Medicare Advantage and the private market, which would improve operational efficiencies for states and health plans, as well as improve the experience of care for individuals who transition between health care coverage options.

The proposed rule promotes state delivery system reform through encouraging initiatives within managed care programs that strive to improve health care outcomes and beneficiary experience while controlling costs. The proposed rule acknowledges the greater demand of mental health and substance abuse disorder services by clarifying that states are permitted to make a monthly capitation payment to a managed care plan for an enrollee that has a short term stay (no more than 15 days) in an institution for mental disease. The proposed rule would require a quality strategy for a state's entire Medicaid program and also establish a Medicaid managed care quality rating system that would include performance information on all health plans and align with the existing rating systems in Medicare Advantage and the Marketplace. By clarifying actuarial soundness requirements, CMS intends to strengthen fiscal and programmatic integrity of Medicaid managed care programs and rate setting. CMS also intends to implement best practices identified in existing managed long-term services and supports programs. The proposed rule would improve the beneficiary experience by making additional information and support systems available to individuals as they enroll in managed care. The proposed rule also supports beneficiaries by strengthening requirements on managed care plans to ensure that covered services are available and that individuals get high-quality, coordinated care through efforts such as strengthening network adequacy. In order to ensure CHIP beneficiaries the same quality and access in managed care programs, where appropriate, CHIP managed care regulations would be largely aligned with the proposed revisions to the Medicaid managed care rules.

BUILDING ENHANCED DATA SYSTEMS

Improving and enhancing Medicaid data systems is an important part of CMS efforts to modernize the program. Better data systems can help both CMS and states measure health care quality and improve program integrity and Medicaid financial management. CMS has encouraged and supported states in their efforts to modernize and improve state Medicaid Management Information Systems, which will produce greater efficiencies and strengthen program integrity. CMS also developed the Transformed Medicaid Statistical Information System (T-MSIS). T-MSIS will facilitate state submission of timely claims data to HHS, expand the MSIS dataset, and allow CMS to review the completeness and quality of State MSIS submittals. CMS will explore using this data for the Medicaid improper payment measurement, evaluating section 1115 waivers and models being tested by the CMS Innovation Center, and to satisfy other HHS requirements. Through the use of

T-MSIS, CMS will not only acquire higher quality data, but will also reduce state data requests. States will move from MSIS to T-MSIS on a rolling basis with the goal of having all states submitting data in the T-MSIS file format by the end of 2015.

STRENGTHENING PROGRAM INTEGRITY

CMS is committed to sound financial management of the Medicaid program and works to ensure that we are good stewards of taxpayer dollars. States and the Federal Government share mutual obligations and accountability for the integrity of the Medicaid program and the development, application, and improvement of program safeguards necessary to ensure proper and appropriate use of both Federal and State dollars. This Federal-State partnership is central to the success of the Medicaid program, and it depends on clear lines of responsibility and shared expectations. Through provisions included in the Affordable Care Act and through CMS regulations, we are enhancing program integrity by strengthening provider and beneficiary eligibility safeguards, as well as by maintaining strong oversight partnerships and data exchanges with states. For example, the Affordable Care Act required CMS to implement risk-based screening of providers and suppliers who want to participate in Medicare, Medicaid, and CHIP.

HHS has implemented a Comprehensive Medicaid Integrity Plan (CMIP), which provides a strategy for CMS to improve Medicaid program integrity for the FY 2014-2018 period.[9] The execution of the strategies in CMIP will improve the ability of state Medicaid agencies and CMS to leverage program data to detect and prevent improper payments, which will strengthen the ability of state Medicaid agencies to safeguard state and Federal Medicaid dollars from diversion into fraud, waste, and abuse. In addition, CMS is working to streamline its assessments of state Medicaid program integrity activities. CMS began conducting comprehensive state program integrity reviews in 2007 on a triennial basis. These reviews play a critical role in how CMS provides assistance to states in their efforts to combat provider fraud and abuse.

CONFRONTING CHALLENGES AND MOVING FORWARD

Throughout its 50-year history, Medicaid has served as an adaptable program, adjusting to national and state-specific needs and meeting the health care needs of children, adults, pregnant women, seniors, and people with disabilities. For these low-income Americans, Medicaid has provided health insurance coverage that is affordable, accessible, and has served as the Nation's major source of long-term care coverage. CMS will continue to work closely with states and other stakeholders to continue to strengthen the Medicaid program in key areas such as modernizing the enrollment process; strengthening delivery systems and managed care; increasing our collection and use of data to make policy and program-management decisions; and enabling individuals with disabilities to live in their homes and communities.

I appreciate the Subcommittee's ongoing interest in the Medicaid program, and look forward to working with you to strengthen and improve Medicaid for the people the program serves.

End Notes

[1] http://www.commonwealthfund.org/publications/issue-briefs/2015/jun/does-medicaid-make-a-d ifference.

[2] http://www.nber.org/papers/w20835.

[3] http://www.medicaid.gov/medicaid-chip-program-information/program-info rmation/download s/april-2015- enrollment-report.pdf.

[4] http://aspe.hhs.gov/health/reports/2015/medicaidexpansion/ibuncompen sate dcare.pdf.

[5] http://www.gallup.com/poll/181664/arkansas-kentucky-improvement-unin su red-rates.aspx 6http://care.diabetesjournals.org/content/38/5/833.long.

[7] http://kff.org/health-reform/issue-brief/medicaid-moving-forward/.

[8] For more information: http://innovation.cms.gov/initiatives/State-Inno vations-Round-Two/ index.html.

[9] http://www.cms.gov/Regulations-and-Guidance/Legislation/DeficitReductionAct/Downloads/c mip2014.pdf.

In: Key Issues Facing Medicaid
Editor: Jimmy Phillips

ISBN: 978-1-63484-647-9
© 2016 Nova Science Publishers, Inc.

Chapter 4

STATEMENT OF ANNE SCHWARTZ, EXECUTIVE DIRECTOR, MEDICAID AND CHIP PAYMENT AND ACCESS COMMISSION (MACPAC). HEARING ON "MEDICAID AT 50: STRENGTHENING AND SUSTAINING THE PROGRAM"[*]

Good morning Chairman Pitts, Ranking Member Green, and Members of the Subcommittee on Health. I am Anne Schwartz, executive director of MACPAC, the Medicaid and CHIP Payment and Access Commission.

As you know, MACPAC is a congressional advisory body charged with analyzing and reviewing Medicaid and State Children's Health Insurance Program (CHIP) policies and making recommendations to Congress, the Secretary of the U.S. Department of Health and Human Services, and the states on issues affecting these programs. Its 17 members, led by Chair Diane Rowland and Vice Chair Marsha Gold, are appointed by the U.S. Government Accountability Office. The insights and expertise I will share this morning reflect the consensus views of the Commission itself. We appreciate the opportunity to share MACPAC's recommendations and work as this committee considers the future of Medicaid.

---

[*] This is an edited, reformatted and augmented version of a statement presented July 8, 2015 before the House Committee on Energy and Commerce, Subcommittee on Health.

Medicaid is a major and important part of the U.S. health care system, covering 72 million people in fiscal year (FY) 2013, more than 20 percent of the U.S. population. The program covers almost half of the nation's births, pays for more than 60 percent of national spending on long-term services and supports (LTSS) to frail elders and other people with disabilities, and accounts for more than a quarter of national spending on treatment for mental health and substance use disorders. In total, it accounts for about 15 percent of national health expenditures, 8.6 percent of federal outlays, and 15.1 percent of spending from state-funded budgets, including state general funds, bonds, and other state funds (which for Medicaid includes provider taxes and local funds that flow through the state budget). It should be noted that while Medicaid has grown as a share of the federal budget, increasing from 1.4 percent of federal outlays in FY 1970 to 8.6 percent in FY 2014, annual growth in Medicaid spending per enrollee has been lower or comparable to Medicare and private insurance since the early 1990s.

While we often compare Medicaid's performance as a payer with other sources of coverage, such as Medicare and employer-sponsored insurance, it is important to recognize Medicaid's unique roles. In addition to providing health insurance to individuals who otherwise may not have access to coverage, it is also a major source of revenue for safety net providers serving both Medicaid beneficiaries and those without insurance. It covers enabling services such as non-emergency transportation and translation services that help beneficiaries access needed health services. Moreover, it wraps around other sources of coverage, including both employer-sponsored insurance and Medicare in its role for 10.7 million dually eligible beneficiaries. Notably, despite the fact that Medicare is the major source of medical coverage for the nation's elderly, it does not cover LTSS. For those in need of long-term care, Medicaid coverage for ongoing nursing facility or other institutional arrangements, home health, personal care, and other home and community-based services (HCBS) is vital to their daily lives.

LOOKING BACK

Since the early 1990s, the Medicaid program has changed in significant ways. During this time period, the country weathered two economic recessions. States responded to budgetary pressures by undertaking modernization efforts and cost containment strategies. As a result, the program has moved from a traditional fee-for-service model to one in which managed care has become the dominant delivery system. More than half of all beneficiaries are now enrolled in comprehensive risk-based plans, and another 20 percent receive some of their benefits through a non-comprehensive managed care arrangement, including primary care case management and limited benefit plans. While initially managed care covered primarily children and their mothers, increasingly managed care is being extended to populations with more complex health needs. Managed care is also transforming the delivery of long-term services and supports. In 2004, just eight states had managed LTSS programs. By the end of this year, more than half of the states are expected to be using managed care models for such services.

The Supreme Court's 1999 decision in *Olmstead v. L.C.* requiring that persons with disabilities be served in the least restrictive environment resulted in a major shift in the provision of long-term services and supports from nursing facilities to home and community-based settings. In FY 1995, 18 percent of Medicaid LTSS spending occurred in a non-institutional setting; by FY 2012, the figure had risen to nearly half.

In the 1990s, congressional action broadened children's coverage through Medicaid and CHIP, and encouraged states to reach out to people eligible but not enrolled in coverage. These actions substantially reduced the share of children without health insurance. In 1997, 22.4 percent of children below the federal poverty level and 22.8 percent of those with family incomes between 100 and 200 percent FPL were uninsured. By 2014, these percentages had dropped to 6.9 percent and 8.9 percent respectively.

More recently, the Patient Protection and Affordable Care Act (ACA, P.L. 111-148, as amended) created new dynamics, allowing states to expand coverage to previously ineligible childless adults and parents. Twenty nine states and the District of Columbia have now expanded their programs, and other states are examining their options. Streamlined eligibility and enrollment processes, including the adoption of modified adjusted gross income (MAGI) as the standard for income determinations, now allow for one-stop shopping for individuals seeking health care coverage. The law also created new options for states for delivery of HCBS, including the Community First Choice program for individuals who are eligible for Medicaid and have incomes below 150 percent FPL but who may not meet institutional level-of-care criteria, or those with such needs whose incomes exceed 150 percent FPL, the

118   Anne Schwartz

Health Homes option, extension and modification of the Money Follows the Person demonstration, and establishment of the state Balancing Incentive Payments program.

LOOKING AHEAD

The 20 years ahead are likely to be similarly dynamic as states experiment with different approaches to delivery system design and payment, including the delivery system reform incentive payment (DSRIP) programs described in MACPAC's June 2015 report to Congress. States are also seeking to provide care more effectively and efficiently for high-cost, high-need individuals such as those with behavioral health conditions and beneficiaries dually eligible for Medicare and Medicaid, also the subject of analysis in our 2015 reports.

Pressure on federal and state budgets creates challenges to ensuring the sustainability of the program and making certain that beneficiaries have access to high-value services that promote their health and ability to function in their communities. These challenges are not unique to Medicaid. Between FY 2014 and FY 2022, annual growth in Medicaid spending per enrollee is projected to average about 4 percent, similar to the rate for Medicare and lower than the rate for private insurance.

MACPAC'S AGENDA

MACPAC's analytic agenda for the year ahead reflects several of these challenges. We will extend the work published in our June report on Medicaid's role for people with behavioral health disorders, focusing on how to improve the delivery of care and better understand models of integration for various subpopulations such as those with serious mental illness. We will also continue to focus on the impact of value-based purchasing initiatives including accountable care organizations, bundled payments, and patient-centered medical homes, and the extent to which these bend the cost curve and improve health.

In the area of access, we will be strengthening and extending our longstanding efforts to measure access to care, an issue now more salient than ever given the Supreme Court's decision in *Armstrong v. Exceptional Child Center* which will put new pressures on the federal government to ensure that Medicaid payment rates are sufficient to ensure access comparable to that of the general population. In addition, we will be examining more closely the extent to which different groups of Medicaid beneficiaries are at risk of access barriers and for which services (for example, specialty care) and the extent to which such barriers can be effectively addressed through Medicaid policy.

Our analyses on the impact of the ACA will include a major effort, as required by Congress, to model the impact of disproportionate share hospital (DSH) payment reductions. Our first report examining the impact that such changes will have on hospitals is due February 1st of next year. In addition, building on our March 2015 report chapter examining premium assistance models in Arkansas and Iowa, we will be also be considering how different approaches to Medicaid expansion affect expenditures and use of services.

At the request of members of this committee and others in Congress, we will analyze and evaluate various policy options to restructure the program's financing. We will be moving to the next chapter in our work on children's coverage, looking ahead to recommend what policies should be in place to assure adequate and affordable coverage for low- and moderate-income children before CHIP funding expires in FY 2017.

Finally we will continue to highlight the importance of having appropriate data available for both policy analysis and program accountability. Since its inaugural report to Congress in March 2011, the Commission has continually called for improvements in the timeliness, quality, and availability of administrative data on Medicaid and CHIP, noting the importance of these data in answering key policy and operational questions that affect beneficiaries, providers, states, and the federal government. As noted in our June 2013 report, given that plans to modernize federal data systems currently rely on a patchwork of program integrity, quality measurement, health information technology, and CHIP reauthorization funds, the Commission is concerned whether available resources are sufficient for this purpose.

MACPAC has also commented on administrative capacity constraints at the federal and state levels that affect the ability to meet program requirements, provide oversight, and take on broader delivery system reforms that promote value and contain costs. As noted in the Commission's June 2014 report, there are few clear performance standards or metrics to assess state capacity, identify gaps in performance, prioritize investments, and identify appropriate responses.

This is an area where we plan to work with state officials and experts in performance management to shed light on promising approaches.

Again, thank you for this opportunity to share the Commission's work with this subcommittee and I am happy to answer any questions.

INDEX

#

2001 recession, 53

A

abuse, 84, 94, 100, 112
access, 2, 5, 6, 7, 11, 17, 18, 20, 21, 23, 24, 25, 28, 36, 38, 47, 58, 59, 60, 61, 62, 67, 78, 91, 94, 95, 97, 98, 99, 100, 101, 104, 108, 109, 111, 116, 118
accountability, 7, 28, 31, 32, 36, 39, 59, 61, 91, 112, 119
accounting, 3, 8, 32, 37, 51, 81, 91
adjustment, 30
Administration for Children and Families, 79
adulthood, 99
adults, vii, 1, 4, 9, 17, 18, 20, 28, 46, 59, 68, 69, 70, 78, 93, 97, 98, 99, 101, 113, 117
advisory body, 115
age, 4, 9, 18, 45, 61, 78, 85, 90, 99, 101
agencies, 39, 79, 85, 86, 105, 112
AIDS, 98
Alaska, 68
American Recovery and Reinvestment Act, 53
American Recovery and Reinvestment Act of 2009, 53
annual rate, 85, 96

assessment, 46, 110
assistive technology, 109
attachment, 96
audit(s), 6, 32, 43, 44, 45, 63, 67
authorit(ies), 5, 36, 39, 40, 58, 60, 65, 88, 91, 96, 101, 108
avoidance, 67
awareness, 47, 103

B

barriers, 119
behaviors, 102
benchmarks, 37, 82
beneficiaries, 36, 66, 89, 91, 93, 94, 97, 99, 100, 102, 103, 104, 105, 106, 107, 108, 109, 110, 111, 116, 117, 118, 119
benefits, 7, 11, 22, 27, 45, 49, 50, 60, 67, 85, 89, 93, 94, 99, 117
births, 88, 103, 104, 116
blood, 99
blood pressure, 99
bonds, 116
breastfeeding, 104
Bureau of Labor Statistics, 58

C

call centers, 100
care model, 104, 105, 117

caregivers, 109
Census, 46, 53, 58
certification, 48
cervical cancer, 98
cesarean section, 104
challenges, 1, 5, 7, 9, 17, 18, 19, 20, 32, 47, 50, 54, 57, 59, 60, 61, 67, 92, 94, 98, 100, 107, 118
childhood, 99
children, vii, 1, 4, 7, 9, 11, 18, 19, 20, 21, 22, 23, 24, 25, 28, 46, 59, 64, 79, 80, 90, 91, 93, 94, 97, 98, 99, 101, 113, 117, 119
cholesterol, 105
chronic diseases, 98
chronic illness, 103
citizenship, 49, 89
classes, 80
clinical application, 61
communit(ies), 4, 10, 11, 61, 89, 91, 99, 100, 104, 105, 106, 108, 109, 110, 113, 116, 117, 118
community-based services (CBS), 4, 61, 91, 108, 109, 110, 116
complexity, 9, 28, 89, 91
compliance, 9, 43, 48, 63, 82, 84
Congress, 3, 5, 8, 9, 32, 38, 39, 53, 55, 62, 63, 65, 77, 84, 85, 92, 93, 115, 118, 119
Congressional Budget Office, 3, 59
consensus, 115
consumers, 85, 100
coordination, 41, 91, 103, 104
cost, 8, 20, 40, 41, 44, 47, 49, 55, 56, 57, 58, 60, 61, 67, 80, 82, 83, 85, 89, 91, 92, 93, 98, 99, 102, 103, 104, 117, 118
cost curve, 118
counseling, 79
covering, 4, 9, 90, 93, 116

D

data collection, 25, 36, 66, 82
data set, 31, 81
database, 48, 50, 67, 84
decay, 23
deficit, 24

demonstrations, 2, 7, 14, 36, 37, 38, 39, 40, 60, 61, 63, 65, 80, 82, 83, 95, 96, 102, 105, 108
dental care, 2, 7, 17, 19, 23, 78
dentist, 23, 64
Department of Health and Human Services, 2, 3, 5, 13, 16, 63, 64, 71, 103, 115
Department of Homeland Security, 84
diabetes, 18, 102, 105
diastolic blood pressure, 105
directors, 38, 52, 61, 66
diseases, 98
disorder, 24, 106, 111
distribution, 10
District of Columbia, 10, 12, 52, 53, 68, 85, 88, 101, 104, 107, 117
diversity, 2, 5, 8, 9, 28, 40, 57, 93
donations, 34
draft, 2, 9, 21, 62
drugs, 10, 11, 61, 86

E

economic downturn, 3, 8, 51, 52, 54, 55, 63, 98
education, 102
elders, 116
eligibility criteria, 17, 89
emergency, 11, 105, 116
employers, 98
employment, 3, 52, 54, 56, 85
enforcement, 94
enrollment, 4, 11, 16, 17, 38, 44, 49, 50, 52, 54, 56, 58, 59, 62, 67, 68, 69, 70, 71, 83, 84, 85, 90, 95, 99, 100, 101, 113, 117
environment, 22, 103, 117
equity, 58
evidence, 6, 37, 48, 80
exclusion, 49, 80, 84
execution, 112
expenditures, 4, 8, 10, 11, 14, 16, 17, 31, 33, 37, 39, 43, 59, 60, 61, 71, 78, 81, 82, 83, 85, 89, 90, 91, 93, 95, 119
expertise, 45, 115

Index

123

F

families, 98
family income, 117
family members, 109
family support, 104
federal assistance, 3, 8, 51, 54
federal funds, 37, 40, 45, 48, 93, 95
federal government, 4, 5, 8, 14, 16, 30, 33, 35, 36, 37, 38, 39, 40, 43, 50, 60, 71, 84, 85, 88, 90, 93, 98, 99, 112, 118, 119
federal law, 33, 80, 83
federal regulations, 50, 84
financial, 8, 29, 44, 48, 49, 51, 89, 92, 93, 98, 100, 107, 108, 111, 112
financial data, 44
financial incentives, 108
financial oversight, 48
financial stability, 98
financial support, 29, 98
fiscal year, 2, 4, 8, 11, 12, 14, 29, 33, 35, 37, 40, 49, 50, 61, 80, 82, 83, 93, 95, 116
fixed rate, 105
flexibility, 5, 14, 29, 33, 89, 98, 105
Food and Drug Administration, 61
forecasting, 81
formula, 3, 8, 14, 16, 17, 51, 53, 54, 55, 56, 57, 63, 71, 90
fraud, 49, 50, 79, 84, 94, 96, 100, 112
funding, 3, 8, 33, 36, 39, 51, 53, 54, 55, 56, 82, 84, 90, 92, 101, 106, 119
funds, 2, 3, 5, 7, 8, 10, 12, 14, 28, 29, 33, 35, 36, 39, 40, 43, 51, 55, 57, 59, 65, 66, 80, 81, 82, 89, 90, 91, 93, 94, 100, 102, 107, 109, 116, 119

G

GAO, 1, 2, 3, 5, 6, 9, 10, 12, 13, 16, 18, 19, 20, 21, 22, 26, 28, 30, 34, 35, 41, 42, 44, 46, 51, 52, 53, 54, 56, 58, 62, 63, 64, 65, 66, 67, 71, 72, 73, 74, 75, 76, 77, 78, 79, 80, 81, 82, 83, 84, 85, 86, 92, 93, 94, 95, 96

General Services Administration, 84
Georgia, 68
gestation, 103
goods and services, 109
governance, 105
governments, 33, 82
grants, 39
growth, 5, 9, 31, 37, 57, 61, 82, 83, 92, 93, 96, 98, 116, 118
growth rate, 37, 82
guidance, 21, 25, 39, 40, 43, 47, 48, 50, 64, 66, 67, 79, 81, 84, 96, 102
guidelines, 82, 90, 98, 109

H

Hawaii, 68
health, vii, 1, 2, 4, 5, 9, 10, 11, 18, 20, 21, 25, 27, 33, 34, 38, 39, 40, 46, 47, 49, 50, 57, 58, 59, 60, 61, 64, 78, 79, 80, 82, 83, 84, 85, 88, 92, 93, 94, 95, 97, 98, 100, 101, 102, 103, 104, 105, 106, 107, 108, 109, 110, 111, 113, 116, 117, 118, 119
health care, vii, 1, 2, 4, 5, 9, 10, 11, 25, 33, 34, 40, 46, 47, 49, 57, 58, 59, 60, 61, 79, 82, 83, 84, 88, 92, 93, 94, 95, 98, 100, 101, 102, 103, 104, 106, 107, 110, 111, 113, 116, 117
health care costs, 58, 98
health care programs, 49
health care system, 5, 88, 102, 103, 116
health condition, 18, 20, 104, 118
health education, 80
health expenditure, 116
health information, 110, 119
health insurance, 38, 46, 58, 60, 85, 88, 97, 98, 113, 116, 117
health problems, 21
health services, 21, 25, 27, 79, 83, 98, 105, 116
heart disease, 105
hemoglobin, 105
HHS, 1, 2, 3, 5, 7, 8, 9, 13, 14, 21, 23, 25, 28, 33, 36, 37, 38, 39, 40, 50, 51, 55, 60, 61, 62, 63, 64, 65, 66, 67, 72, 73, 74, 78,

79, 80, 82, 83, 84, 85, 93, 94, 103, 111, 112
hiring, 45
historical data, 38
history, 80, 113
HIV, 98
homes, 4, 105, 107, 113, 118
hospice, 11
House, 87, 97, 115
household income, 84
housing, 83
hub, 50, 84
hyperactivity, 24

I

identification, 80
immigration, 49, 89
improvements, 2, 8, 24, 51, 64, 98, 101, 102, 119
incarceration, 84
income, vii, 1, 4, 9, 39, 40, 56, 57, 58, 78, 79, 88, 90, 91, 97, 98, 101, 113, 117, 119
income determination, 117
individuals, vii, 1, 2, 4, 5, 7, 8, 9, 12, 14, 16, 17, 18, 19, 20, 23, 39, 40, 41, 49, 50, 52, 58, 71, 77, 78, 79, 80, 83, 84, 85, 90, 93, 94, 99, 101, 108, 109, 110, 111, 113, 116, 117, 118
industry, 105
information technology, 3, 45, 101
innovator, 102
institutions, 10, 61, 109
integration, 106, 118
integrity, 2, 6, 8, 38, 41, 43, 44, 45, 47, 59, 61, 62, 67, 91, 94, 100, 102, 110, 111, 112, 119
intellectual disabilities, 11
intervention, 101
investment(s), 67, 99, 119
Iowa, 60, 68, 83, 85, 102, 119
issues, vii, 1, 2, 3, 5, 6, 9, 23, 31, 32, 49, 50, 60, 62, 71, 72, 95, 107, 115

L

labor market, 54
laboratory tests, 80
landscape, 92
LDL, 105
leadership, 47
learning, 45, 107
legislation, 16, 32, 71
light, 61, 120
local government, 29, 30, 31, 33, 36, 82, 90, 93
long-term services, 3, 4, 10, 60, 88, 89, 106, 110, 111, 116, 117
long-term services and supports (LTSS), 3, 4, 10, 60, 78, 88, 89, 91, 92, 106, 109, 110, 111, 116, 117
Louisiana, 69

M

magnitude, 54
majority, 21, 79, 110
management, 11, 16, 50, 57, 71, 79, 91, 92, 100, 103, 104, 111, 112, 113, 117, 120
Maryland, 69
matter, 62
measurement, 107, 111, 119
Medicaid, vii, 1, 2, 3, 4, 5, 6, 7, 8, 9, 10, 11, 12, 13, 14, 16, 17, 18, 19, 20, 21, 22, 23, 24, 26, 27, 28, 29, 30, 31, 32, 33, 34, 35, 36, 37, 38, 39, 40, 41, 42, 43, 44, 45, 46, 47, 48, 49, 50, 51, 52, 53, 54, 55, 56, 57, 58, 59, 60, 61, 62, 63, 64, 65, 66, 67, 68, 69, 70, 71, 72, 73, 74, 75, 76, 77, 78, 79, 80, 81, 82, 83, 84, 85, 86, 87, 88, 89, 90, 91, 92, 93, 94, 95, 96, 97, 98, 99, 100, 101, 102, 103, 104, 105, 106, 107, 108, 109, 110, 111, 112, 113, 115, 116, 117, 118, 119
medical, 17, 18, 20, 49, 81, 82, 89, 99, 104, 105, 116, 118
medical assistance, 82, 89
medical care, 17, 18, 20, 99, 104

Index

Medicare, 1, 3, 4, 5, 13, 30, 44, 50, 60, 63, 64, 67, 75, 76, 77, 78, 79, 80, 84, 86, 88, 89, 96, 97, 98, 103, 106, 107, 108, 110, 111, 112, 116, 118
medication, 21, 24, 79
medicine, 18, 61
mellitus, 105
mental health, 7, 11, 19, 20, 21, 39, 79, 88, 106, 111, 116
mental illness, 118
methodology, 6, 67, 84, 91
Mexico, 69, 83
Missouri, 69, 82, 104
models, 7, 25, 28, 60, 64, 92, 103, 105, 107, 108, 111, 118, 119
modernization, 101, 117
modifications, 90, 109
modules, 48
Montana, 69

N

National Survey, 79
needy, vii, 1, 4, 9
neglect, 84, 94
neutral, 37, 39, 82
nursing, 4, 11, 33, 35, 61, 80, 89, 116, 117
nursing home, 4, 33, 61

O

obesity, 18
officials, 1, 5, 7, 19, 20, 25, 32, 38, 43, 48, 64, 78, 80, 81, 84, 120
Oklahoma, 70
operating costs, 31
operating system, 45
operations, 14, 101
opportunities, 32, 54, 92, 102, 108, 109
oral health, 80
outpatient, 4, 11, 61, 108
oversight, vii, 1, 2, 3, 5, 6, 7, 8, 9, 13, 21, 25, 28, 29, 32, 36, 41, 43, 45, 47, 48, 57, 59, 60, 61, 64, 67, 79, 82, 92, 93, 95, 96, 112, 119
ownership, 30, 49, 67, 80

P

parents, 9, 80, 90, 117
participants, 105
patient care, 47
per capita income, 8, 14, 57, 58, 85, 90
persons with disabilities, 9, 78, 117
pharmaceuticals, 61
physical health, 104
physicians, 11, 19, 21, 79
platform, 98
playing, 97
policy, 2, 7, 28, 29, 33, 36, 37, 38, 43, 55, 58, 59, 65, 66, 81, 82, 85, 92, 98, 113, 119
policy choice, 55
policy making, 59
policy options, 119
policymakers, 36, 55
population, vii, 1, 3, 4, 9, 11, 28, 54, 56, 57, 58, 59, 61, 78, 82, 84, 85, 90, 91, 93, 99, 102, 107, 116, 119
portfolio, 96
poverty, 3, 10, 85, 90, 93, 101, 117
precedent, 38
pregnancy, 104
prescription drugs, 10, 61
President, 82, 83, 93
primary data, 31
principles, 83, 110
protection, 98
prototype, 54, 55, 56
psychiatry, 21
psychotropic medications, 21, 22, 64, 79
Puerto Rico, 104

Q

quality assurance, 25
quality standards, 105

R

real time, 14, 85
recession, 53, 56, 92
recommendations, 2, 5, 8, 23, 33, 38, 40, 41, 43, 45, 47, 51, 54, 61, 62, 63, 106, 115
recovery, 54, 92, 104
reform(s), 93, 95, 97, 99, 102, 103, 105, 106, 107, 110, 113, 118, 119
regulations, 50, 83, 91, 110, 111, 112
regulatory requirements, 83
reliability, 81, 103
relief, 36
requirement(s), 9, 12, 13, 14, 32, 36, 44, 48, 49, 59, 60, 61, 81, 82, 83, 84, 85, 88, 89, 94, 101, 106, 109, 111, 119
researchers, 99
resources, 8, 21, 44, 45, 51, 55, 57, 58, 59, 108, 119
response, 3, 23, 25, 41, 50, 53, 54, 55, 63, 83
responsiveness, 54
revenue, 52, 53, 54, 88, 116
rewards, 103
risk, 5, 9, 16, 22, 38, 40, 43, 46, 48, 50, 57, 68, 69, 70, 71, 93, 103, 104, 105, 110, 112, 117, 119
rules, 40, 80, 89, 95, 98, 99, 100, 110, 111

S

safety, 4, 92, 94, 103, 116
savings, 14, 103, 107, 108
scaling, 56
school, 98
scope, 6, 78, 89
secondary education, 4
Secretary of HHS, 36, 38, 83, 94, 96
security, 98
services, 2, 4, 7, 8, 9, 10, 11, 14, 18, 19, 21, 23, 24, 25, 27, 28, 29, 30, 31, 38, 40, 47, 49, 51, 53, 55, 57, 58, 61, 64, 78, 80, 81, 83, 84, 89, 94, 95, 98, 99, 100, 102, 104, 105, 106, 108, 109, 110, 111, 116, 117, 118, 119
simulations, 107
Social Security, 9, 36, 49, 50, 84, 92, 94
Social Security Administration, 49, 50, 84
social support, 104
South Dakota, 70, 82
specialists, 94
speech, 11
spending, 2, 4, 7, 10, 11, 12, 16, 17, 28, 29, 31, 32, 36, 37, 38, 39, 40, 41, 58, 59, 60, 61, 63, 65, 66, 68, 69, 70, 71, 81, 82, 83, 88, 92, 96, 105, 109, 110, 116, 117, 118
stability, 3, 9, 51, 54
stakeholders, 65, 102, 106, 113
state(s), vii, 1, 2, 3, 4, 5, 7, 8, 9, 10, 11, 12, 13, 14, 16, 17, 19, 20, 21, 23, 24, 25, 28, 29, 30, 31, 32, 33, 35, 36, 37, 38, 39, 40, 41, 43, 44, 45, 46, 47, 48, 49, 50, 51, 52, 53, 54, 55, 56, 57, 58, 59, 60, 61, 62, 63, 64, 65, 66, 67, 68, 69, 70, 71, 78, 79, 80, 81, 82, 83, 84, 85, 86, 88, 89, 90, 91, 92, 93, 94, 97, 98, 99, 100, 101, 102, 103, 104, 105, 106, 107, 108, 109, 110, 111, 112, 113, 115, 116, 117, 118, 119
state innovation, 106
state oversight, 40, 43, 47, 60
statistics, 78
stress, 9, 51
structural reforms, 109
structure, 14
substance abuse, 88, 111
substance use, 106, 116
substance use disorders, 106, 116
suppliers, 112
Supreme Court, 90, 117, 118
sustainability, 118

T

target, 106
Task Force, 106
tax credits, 85
tax evasion, 94
taxes, 33, 34, 36, 82, 90, 93, 116

Index

taxpayers, 3, 5, 6, 55, 62, 92, 93
technical assistance, 13, 21
technical comments, 2, 9, 62
technical support, 107
technological advances, 61
technolog(ies), 4, 58, 59, 61, 110, 119
tension, 5
territory, 88
testing, 32, 60, 103, 107, 110
theft, 94
therapy, 11, 79
tooth, 23
total costs, 31
trade, 56
trade-off, 56
training, 25, 83
transformation, 3, 9, 62, 106, 107
translation, 116
transparency, 6, 7, 28, 29, 32, 36, 38, 40, 99
transportation, 18, 109, 116
Treasury, 58
treatment, 20, 24, 44, 64, 79, 88, 89, 98, 116

U

unemployment rate, 56
uninsured, 2, 29, 80, 81, 98, 99, 101, 102, 117
United States, 1, 88, 102
updating, 99

V

validation, 81
variables, 55
variations, 8, 51
vision, 107
vulnerability, 94

W

wages, 56, 57, 99
waiver, 85, 88, 93, 101, 108
Washington, 70, 72, 73, 74, 75, 76, 77, 78, 79, 80, 81, 82, 83, 84, 85, 86, 101, 108, 109
waste, 94, 100, 112
wealth, 55
web, 72
welfare, 64
Wisconsin, 70
workers, 83, 109
workforce, 83
working families, 98, 100

Y

yield, 32